A YEAR WITH YOUR PUPPY

by Penny Dent

Dentbros Dogs

Dentbros.co.uk

Copyright © Penny Dent

All rights reserved

Acknowledgements

In 2020, during the first Lockdown, I began a fantastic photography course, called 'A Year With My Camera' by Emma Davies. Each week there was an email, with some instruction and some homework to do. You posted the homework into a Facebook group, with explanation, if you wanted to. It was a brilliant course and concept. I can take better photos now. This book is inspired by Emma's course.

Dedication

This book is dedicated to my husband Chris, who loves all the dogs as much as I do.

And to the boy, Quin.

A YEAR WITH YOUR PUPPY

Introduction 5
FOUR WAYS TO GET A PERFECT DOG 8
SEVEN WAYS TO BE A PERFECT DOG OWNER 11
WEEK 0: YOUR PUPPY ARRIVES! 15
WEEK 1: TEACH YOUR PUPPY ITS NAME - INFORMATION 19
WEEK 2: PLAY WITH YOUR PUPPY - TRAINING 21
WEEK 3: BITING PUPPY? - PROBLEM 25
WEEK 4: FIRST WALK - INFORMATION 28
WEEK 5: SOCIALISATION - TRAINING 31
WEEK 6: JUMPING UP - PROBLEM 34
WEEK 7: TRAVELLING - INFORMATION 37
WEEK 8: PLAYDATE! - TRAINING 40
WEEK 9: TOILETING – PROBLEM 43
WEEK 10: DOG TOYS - INFORMATION 48
WEEK 11: WAIT! - TRAINING 52
WEEK 12: BARKING AND HOWLING - PROBLEM 56
WEEK 13: DOGs AND CHILDREN – INFORMATION 60
WEEK 14: ON LEAD WALKING – TRAINING 63
WEEK 15: PULLING AND LUNGING ON LEAD – PROBLEM 67
WEEK 16: KEEP REWARDING - INFORMATION 71
WEEK 17: RECALL REVISITED - TRAINING 74
WEEK 18: LEAVE IT! - PROBLEM 78
WEEK 19: VET VISITS – INFORMATION 81
WEEK 20: FETCH THE BALL! – TRAINING 85
WEEK 21: GUARDING FOOD/TOYS – PROBLEM 90
WEEK 22: GROOMING YOUR DOG – INFORMATION 94
WEEK 23: DOWN! – TRAINING 98
WEEK 24: DISOBEDIENCE - PROBLEM 101
WEEK 25: THE TEENAGE PHASE - INFORMATION 106
WEEK 26: CELEBRATING 6 MONTHS! 109
WEEK 27: BOREDOM FIGHTING – PROBLEM 114
WEEK 28: CRATES – INFORMATION 118

- WEEK 29: TRICKS – TRAINING 121
- WEEK 30: REVIEW THE PROBLEMS – PROBLEM 125
- WEEK 31: FOOD – INFORMATION 129
- WEEK 32: RECALL AGAIN – TRAINING 133
- WEEK 33: REACTIVITY – PROBLEM 137
- WEEK 34: NEUTERING – INFORMATION 141
- WEEK 35: SOCIALISING ON WALKS – TRAINING 146
- WEEK 36: CAT CHASING – PROBLEM 149
- WEEK 37: GOING ON HOLIDAY – INFORMATION 152
- WEEK 38: STOP THE DOG – TRAINING 155
- WEEK 39: SETTLE DOWN – PROBLEM 158
- WEEK 40: SHOWING – INFORMATION 161
- WEEK 41: SCENTWORK – TRAINING 165
- WEEK 42: OFF LEAD WALKING – PROBLEM 168
- WEEK 43: HEALTH TESTING – INFORMATION 172
- WEEK 44: HOOPERS – TRAINING 176
- WEEK 44: FIRST BIRTHDAY – CELEBRATING! 180
- WEEK 45: BREED TRAITS – PROBLEM 183
- WEEK 46: DOG HEALTH – INFORMATION 187
- WEEK 47: AGILITY – TRAINING 191
- WEEK 48: TEMPERAMENT IN BREEDS – PROBLEM 195
- WEEK 49: VACCINATIONS – INFORMATION 198
- WEEK 50: SEPARATION ANXIETY – TRAINING 202
- WEEK 51: CONTACT WITH YOUR BREEDER 206
- WEEK 52: CELEBRATING A YEAR WITH YOUR PUPPY! 210

Introduction

In June 2021, I kept my 7th puppy, Quin. He's the 9th Border Collie I've had over the past 30 years, as I have also re-homed a couple. Quin is also the 5th puppy I've bred and kept, which was part of the inspiration behind his name.

Me and my dogs

I've had dogs for most of my life and apart from a Cocker Spaniel we had until I was ten years old, these dogs have been Border Collies, in various shapes and sizes. My mum bred from her dogs for fun and I decided to continue that tradition. However, because I was a business person and entrepreneur, I decided to do it to the very best of my ability, becoming a responsible, Kennel Club Assured Breeder from day one.

The first and only dog I bought as a puppy, from a stranger, was Sunny, who came to us in August 2006, at the age of six weeks. She was an absolutely brilliant dog in so many ways and the beginning of my legacy. I started doing agility with her and she taught me that agility is great fun, but very challenging! Sunny was a fantastic dog to begin my breeding journey, producing 22 gorgeous puppies in three litters. I was also lucky enough to be mentored by the owner of the first stud dog I used.

I kept Luna from Sunny's first litter and then when Luna had her first litter, I kept Aura. Three generations, so far so good. My plan was to keep a pup from each dog, each generation. I planned to have a boy at some point, living nearby, whom I could use for stud. Lovely. Of course things don't go according to plan and there have been many hiccups and challenges along the way! I planned to have one litter per year; in 13 years I have had 12 litters, but it has been anything but straightforward.

We currently have six dogs, including Luna and Aura, mother and daughter, aged 12 and 10. Luna is diabetic, with cataracts, so is a bit of a frail old lady. Aura had one litter and one of those pups developed epilepsy, meaning no more pups from her. She's been a fantastic agility dog, winning at grade 5, a massive achievement for me and her.

Busy – my dog of a lifetime. She decided to stay; I wasn't meant to keep her. She has been absolutely brilliant in so many ways. Initially an 'unregistered' Working Sheepdog, I transferred her to the breed register and she has had three amazing litters of pups. I kept Ounce from her first litter, my purple puppy. Then Quin from her third litter, the boy.

Finally, (for now) I have kept Ounce's daughter, Murmur, another lilac girl. She and Quin are not that closely related, as Ounce and Quin have different sires and Murmur has a completely different line on her dad's side. So hopefully Quin and Murmur will have pups of their own, one day.

Quin, Aura, Ounce, Murmur, Busy and Luna

Owning dogs is a constant joy, full of heartache. Breeding is even more of this. I don't recommend becoming a breeder, yet, we need many more dogs bred with love and purpose. We need people to choose to have dogs that have been bred with care and awareness.

I am a very experienced Border Collie owner, but that does not necessarily make me an experienced dog owner. Of course I have come into contact with many dogs over the years and I have had lots of dogs stay in my home. However, there are some breeds of dog that remain a mystery to me. I haven't spent a lot of time with any brachycephalic dogs, so if you have a Pug, or a French Bulldog, this book is probably not going to be that useful to you. Health is my primary concern – I want all my dogs to live long and happy lives. Otherwise, it should be a good resource to help you navigate your first experience of owning a dog.

How to use this book

I've written this course alongside owning Quin during his first year. As with learning any new skill, owning and training a puppy is not a linear process. You need lots of information and hard work at the start, which you gradually consolidate over a long period of time.

Traditional puppy training courses typically last around 6 weeks, with most people missing one or two classes. These days we usually have access to online support and there are sometimes written notes. But once you've attended these classes, you might think you are up and running. Just like having a child, it is not that simple. You will go backwards some weeks and you will definitely need to re-visit some areas several times.

I've written in a 3 week cycle, covering:

- **Information**
- **Training**
- **Problem behaviour.**

Each week you read the lesson, then think about how that affects your relationship with your dog. There will be Weekly Focus Challenge to do. You can share the results of your efforts on social media. You can write up notes on how it is going and stick photos of your dog in this book. It's a record of your progress. All the information is also on the Dentbros Dogs website: Dentbros.co.uk

Before we start the lessons, let's think about how to get a perfect dog? And how to be a perfect dog owner? It's simple really..

FOUR WAYS TO GET A PERFECT DOG

How to make your dog perfect

If you have a dog already, you might think they are perfect. I do think that Ounce is pretty perfect. She's certainly pretty! I love her so much, almost more than my sons and my husband (well I couldn't love her more than them, could I?) Is she perfect though? Is anyone really perfect?

Before you get a dog, you have a picture in your mind of 'life with a dog'. It includes long country walks, kicking up the leaves, with your dog trotting at your side. Is the dog running around off lead, but quickly returning to you when you call them? Or do you imagine a dog like Fenton? He's the dog who chased the deer in Richmond Park, with his owner running desperately after him, shouting his name and swearing.

Your 'perfect dog' picture might have you sitting on the sofa in front of a fire, with your dog's head resting lovingly on your knee, while you stroke him. Is the dog farting? No, didn't think so. Is your dog sitting ON you, so that you can't really see the TV?

When you have children, they usually want a dog. They imagine a cuddly, fluffy puppy, who snuggles up to them and plays games with them. Perhaps they will be dressed up and pushed around. Or they will run around with the children in the garden. Do they see the puppy chewing up a favourite teddy? Or their shoe? Is their puppy being sick on their bedroom carpet?

Here are my 4 key points to help you prepare for life with a dog:

1. **Be realistic**

Get real. A dog is not a toy. Nor are they a person. A puppy that is cuddly at four weeks does not stay that way. So by the time your puppy arrives home with you, they bite – a lot. The only way to stop this is to manage the behaviour, through distraction and plenty of downtime.

You will need a crate or cage to keep your puppy out of danger while you are not actively watching them. A dog run, or playpen, is ideal to help you manage your puppy. You can make sure they are safe, not chewing up the house, but they have room to run about and play.

2. **Be realistic**

A friend with a puppy and a young dog shared a picture of both dogs covered in mud, having been digging in the garden. What a brilliant game for a dog! She did see the funny side of it, but also said "they know they are not supposed to do it". Er, no. Dogs do NOT understand the difference between right and wrong.

A dog will dig. They will chew. They will destroy things. That is how they work. I was reminded of a little quiz I wrote a while ago about when you should punish your dog. When Busy was a pup she chewed a hole in my curtain. I moved the curtain. She chewed another one. I moved that one. She did it TWICE MORE! Why didn't I learn the first time? Silly me.

3. Be realistic

Dogs need stimulation and exercise. If you leave a dog on their own at home all day, don't expect them to be a model of perfection. I have written about separation anxiety and there are many sources of information and advice covering this topic.

Dogs do naturally want to be lying at your feet all day long. But they don't *have* to do this. You need a lifestyle that is manageable for you and your dog. Being consistent is perhaps the best thing you can do, whether that is going out for 6 hours a day or just popping out now and again.

If you work away from the home, it is pretty straightforward to find a good dog walker. You need someone who understands dogs and is able to come regularly. A dog walker also has the advantage of walking a number of compatible dogs together, which ensures additional interaction and engagement.

4. Be realistic

Hopefully by now you have realised that getting a dog is NOT a perfect experience. It will only live up to expectations if your expectations are pretty low (and realistic!) You need to imagine the mess, the mud, the wees, the poos, the chewing and digging, the hair. Make sure you include plenty of disaster and a fair amount of heartache.

When I receive an enquiry from someone, I send them an Application Form. I ask them what their selection criteria are for their dog. They must tell me what kind of dog they want, so I can see if they are being realistic and *specific* about what they want. Do they know that they want a particular breed and why? Have they done some research about what makes their breed so special? Please read my breed blog for ideas on what makes dog breeds different? Or checkout the Kennel Club website, which has masses of information.

I ask people what is the best and worst thing about having a dog. My favourite answer is "getting distracted from chores because all you'd want to do is play with your dog". Dogs definitely are a good reason not to get on – cuddles and play are always available!

Of course the actual worst thing is when they are ill and dying – they're not here for long and losing your dog will break your heart, I promise you that.

It is hard to imagine something we haven't had and often the reality does not match our expectations. If you feel overwhelmed, there is plenty of help out there. It is *essential* to get support from a good dog trainer. I love a trainer that focuses on building a community of people going through the same pain and sharing solutions to all the common problems.

It is hard, having a dog. Not just a puppy, any dog. There is a period of adjustment and sometimes it just doesn't work out. Much better to admit defeat and find a better home for your dog, than to keep struggling and making you and your dog miserable. I'm not going to say that all problems can be dealt with, because some things are just too difficult to solve.

Is it worth it?

Yes. Yes. Yes. A million times yes. Having a dog will improve your life. For better and worse. For richer for poorer (definitely poorer). In sickness and health. Till death us do part. The joy of having a dog is hard to imagine, but once experienced, almost impossible to live without.

When people say to me "I wanted to wait until the time was right", it makes me sad. There is no better time to get a dog than right now. Because dogs do make things better, especially in troubled times. Good luck with your dog!

SEVEN WAYS TO BE A PERFECT DOG OWNER

How to give your dog its best life

With so many first time dog owners appearing during the pandemic, it is hard to recognise just what it takes to do the best you can for your dog. I know people who absolutely adore their dogs, but they do not necessarily have all the right attributes that their dog would want.

I'm going to start off by saying – buy the right dog! That doesn't mean the most expensive, or the one I like (Border Collie). It's what's right *for you*. Choose the right breed and buy from the right breeder. Or get a rescue. I don't mind. It's you that will be living with them for the next 10-15 years. That's almost certainly longer than you'll have your car or your sofa. So it's worth spending a bit of time getting the right one, isn't it? After that, it's up to you..

Here are my top tips:

1. Interact with your dog

Talk to them, play with them, stroke them. You'd be amazed how many people like having a dog around the place, but don't actually engage with them. NB: Don't cuddle your dog unless they ask to be cuddled. Above all, be there for your dog so it doesn't need to rush up to other dogs and people. Your dog should NOT be desperately attention-seeking. They should be happy with its own family.

2. Be present as much as possible

Dogs are sociable and like hanging out together. If you're going to be out all day, make sure you do plenty with your dog when you're in. Hire a good dog walker, who walks dogs in groups. Have another dog. Or a cat.

I'm not saying you can't have a dog if you work. We all have to work at some stage in our lives and I don't think people should deny themselves a dog just because they are out. Dogs sleep for the majority of the day anyway, provided they have had a good walk in the morning and some play, training and interaction later on.

3. Groom your dog

Check your dog over daily for parasites, grass seeds, sores etc. Just stroke them! Brush when you can, but often. Little and often works wonders. Even if you dog has long hair, tackling it for 5 minutes a day can make a big difference.

Many of the poodle crossbreeds need regular professional grooming, which does take time and effort to organise and of course costs money! Take that into consideration when choosing the right dog for you? Don't wait until it is a horrible matted mess that has to be shaved to the skin. We have created dogs in different shapes and sizes, so it is our responsibility to care for them properly.

4. Feed your dog sensibly

A well-balanced diet makes for a happy dog. Pay attention to the level of activity of your dog, rather than what the bag says. Are they active enough? Or too hyper? Too fat? Or too thin? You should be able to feel your dog's ribs, not see them.

We all know that obesity causes terrible health problems, so why inflict that on your dog? 'Just a few treats' is no good if your dog suffers as a result. You have the power to control your dog's food intake and therefore to manage its health proactively. Pay attention.

If you have more than one dog, don't think you can feed them all the same food and don't just chuck the food down and walk away. Control the food you give and watch how it is eaten.

Manage it. Personally, I feed a nutritionally balanced kibble because it works for my dogs. I am not knowledgeable enough to feed them food I have concocted myself. And I can't be bothered! It's easy to feed ourselves rubbish, but why should our dogs have to suffer? Raw food carries bacteria which may be leading to antibiotic resistance, which could be fatal for us all. I do not recommend this.

5. Walk your dog

Walk your dog slowly, so they can sniff and experience the world around it. An hour wandering and sniffing is far better than a pavement trudge several times a day. Don't take them for a run! Dogs don't naturally go 'out for a run' it's not really their thing. They might run around chasing each other in a game, or chasing prey, but it's not really necessary for our dogs. Let them be active in their own space, at their own pace.

Doing the same walk every day is useless – dogs need variety. And of course Let. Them. Off. Lead. You wouldn't go for a walk with a blindfold on. Don't torture your dog – here's a lovely place you can't experience, because I am holding onto you! Here are dogs to say hello to, or be frightened of, but I am hanging on to you so you can't deal with that yourself. Teach your dog how to behave when they are out and about and they can enjoy a relaxing walk. Which brings me on to..

6. **Train your dog!**

Teach your dog to come when you call them. Stand in a different room from your dog and call it. Do they come? If they're barking at a squirrel in the garden and you call them, do they come? If you open the fridge door, does your dog suddenly appear? Hmm, maybe a bit more work on recall is required… It is absolutely NOT difficult, nor is it rocket science. It just takes effort. And lots of practice. With cheese.

You don't have to teach tricks to your dog, but it's fun to engage your brain and theirs. Going to classes can be about focusing on your dog and sharing your experiences with others. Teaching your dog manners will save you both a lot of heartache. Basically, the more effort you make, the more you will enjoy your dog.

7. **Say goodbye with dignity**

Don't put your dog through complex or invasive treatments, especially if they are a reasonable age and have had a good life. Let them go, with love. And be there to hold them as they do. It's hard to part with your best friend and constant companion, but don't make them suffer because you don't want to say goodbye? If you love them, let them go.

They make us laugh, they are there for us, bringing so much joy. Don't they deserve a good life? These points should all have been so obvious they don't need saying, but can you tick them all?

Weekly Focus Challenge

- Think about why you chose the dog you chose? What was it you liked about their breed?
- Why did you choose the breeder you bought your puppy from? What criteria did you have?
- What did you think of the puppy's mum? Was she what you were expecting?
- Now think about your plans for your dog? What are you going to do with it? Will you go to puppy classes? Are you hoping to do a dog activity in the future?
- How often will you walk your dog? Whereabouts will you go?
- What behaviour issues do you anticipate? What do you think will be the biggest problems with your dog?
- What will be the best thing about having your dog?
- What arrangements do you have in place for when you are away? When you are at work?
- What are you worried about?

You can write down the answers to some or all of these questions here:

WEEK 0: YOUR PUPPY ARRIVES!

Preparation and equipment

Before your puppy has arrived in your home, they have already made big changes to your life! You have planned to get them, chosen them, seen them and made changes to your home. You will have gone out and bought 'stuff' for them and set everything up ready. I remember visiting a couple of people before their first dog arrived and it was laughable (for me) how they imagine their life with their dog was going to be.

I recommend the following equipment:

- Dog crate and run
- Bedding, such as vet bed
- Collar and lead, with identity tag
- Bowls for food and water
- Dog toys
- Food and treats
- Car crate, guard or harness
- Poo bags
- Grooming equipment, shampoo and toothpaste

You can go on forever buying things for your dog, but the above are all pretty essential. I recommend talking to the dog's breeder about where to buy all of these from. They will often have top tips about what to buy and may have discount codes or recommended suppliers. My website has details about all of these things.

Making your home safe

Before your puppy arrives home you need to make it a safe space for them. You need to decide where they will spend most of their time and prepare that area. Check for wiring that they can get to and move this. Remove toys, plants, shoes etc, at least for the first few months.

You shouldn't let your puppy go up and down stairs, so think about the best way to stop them from doing this. You might want to section off part of the garden, so that the puppy doesn't dig up your favourite plants, or eat the poisonous ones!

I highly recommend setting up a run, so that you have somewhere safe for the puppy to play when you go to the toilet! Or have to get on with something. You will quickly learn how much you can trust your dog to hang out around you and how much you need to watch and engage with them.

Introducing your puppy to the family

When the puppy arrives home, everyone will be VERY excited! That's understandable, but it can be overwhelming for the puppy. Try to manage this, if possible? Don't invite loads of friends and family round, at least for the first few days. Give yourself time and space to settle and get to know each other.

If you have other pets, introduce these to your puppy calmly and slowly. Manage your expectations – they are not going to be friends straight away. Older dogs in particular will NOT thank you for bringing home a puppy and will probably hate it for several weeks. They should come round eventually, if you manage the interaction carefully and with respect. Cats need to be given time and space too. Most cats can live perfectly happily with dogs, but initially they need to be able to get away and not be hassled. There is a section on cats and dogs for more information.

Children should learn to manage themselves around the puppy. They should not be allowed to pester it constantly - let the puppy come to them for play and attention. If the puppy starts biting excessively they are overtired and need a chance to rest.

Feeding and toileting

Do not expect your puppy to be toilet trained! It takes quite a few weeks to learn the difference between inside and outside. They are also too young to have good bladder control, so when they need to go it will just happen! The more effort you make to work on this the quicker it will happen, but patience is definitely required.

Similarly, your puppy may be unsettled for a few days and have an upset tummy. This might be from travelling or just from adjusting to the new surroundings. They may be off their food, even though it is the same food the breeder gave them. It's fine. Keep offering small amounts of food. Don't leave it down, remove it after a few minutes and then offer again later or discard and start again. Talk to the breeder or your vet if problems persist.

The first night

People get hung up on the trauma of a puppy going off to their new home and coping with being on their own. If a puppy has been lovingly bred in the breeder's home, they won't find the transition that difficult. They will be tired, for one thing, after travelling and exploring and playing. They should be used to being in a crate and to being left, away from their mum.

Once you have had a last wander around the garden and hopefully done a final wee and a poo, pop your puppy into their crate and then sit quietly nearby whilst they fall asleep. When they are settled, leave them to it. If the crate is covered and has a bit of bedding with a familiar smell from mum on it, the puppy should be quite content.

Puppies are not usually 'dry' at night for a few more weeks, so you might need to let them out in the middle of the night. If you set up a run, with the crate open so that they can get out and go on the newspaper, that won't be needed and they are better off left in peace. If you do decide to get up and toilet them, make sure it is quiet and boring.

You will need to get up early though! Puppies do not wait until 8am to start their day – when it's light, we get up! Having said that, you can usually get away with getting up to toilet, have breakfast and a bit of a play, followed by another sleep.

Good luck with everything and away we go – your journey with your puppy has begun!

Weekly Focus Challenge

Have you got everything you need before your puppy comes home? Are you managing your expectations? How do you plan to keep your puppy safe in your home? Where are they going to be left alone? How are they going to travel in the car? How much time have you set aside to look after them for the first few days and weeks?

Share a picture of your puppy looking adorable and cute. Write about how you got on with the challenge below.

WEEK 1: TEACH YOUR PUPPY ITS NAME - INFORMATION

The key words

My mum taught me that there are only two words a puppy needs to know: his name and 'NO!' These days we are a bit more progressive and try to focus on the positive behaviour we do want. So I want to teach him 'Yes!' rather than no, but the latter will inevitably be said as well!

When I have a litter of puppies, I do try using their names as much as possible, but if I call one, they all come! So as soon as I had just Quin, I started to make sure I called him.

I call out 'Quin' then when he looks, (or appears) I call 'Quin come' in a stupidly high-pitched voice. When he comes, I 'draw him in' with my hands, until he is sitting at my feet looking up at me. Then I say 'yes!' and give him a treat. I try to give him two tiny bits of treat, one from each hand. Jackpot!

Practice makes perfect

How often do you think I do this? Once a day? Every now and then? Possibly 10-20 times PER DAY. EVERY SINGLE DAY. The more I do it, the more likely he is to respond.

Is it OK to call him without treats? Er no. What I'm going for is developing a 'Pavlovian response'. If I describe a pizza to you, with oozing cheese and juicy tomato sauce, on a crispy dough base, will your mouth start watering? Mine did! I have that response because I have eaten enough pizza to be able to imagine eating it again.

I want to create that response in my puppy. I want him to hear his name and imagine he is getting a treat! I need it to happen enough times that he makes that instant link. The more practice we do, the stronger his response to his name will be.

Tasty treats

It's no good just giving him a bit of his ordinary food for this. He needs sweeties! Not too big, he's only a baby! Not to rich, or too sweet, too crumbly for you to manage. They must be easy to hold and feed. Personally, I use 'Wagg's Training Treats', because the dogs love them, they are easy to handle and they are cheap and easy to buy. You can also use cheese, or sausage, or liver cake, or bits of chicken, or any one of a million tasty bits of food, as long as they are safe for puppies.

Play away

I have also taught Quin to play with me this week, using a tuggy toy. I think I'll talk more about that next week though. If you have a puppy and you practice recall 100 times this week, that is a good start! I also want to mention that you do need time to spend with your puppy, away from distractions and especially away from other dogs. If you have other young dogs and they spend hours playing every day, that's lovely. But you may then find the puppy is too tired to concentrate when you want to spend time training.

A puppy can only concentrate for 5 minutes, but you do need them to be alert enough to do that. So make sure they have some down time before you ask them to focus.

Older dogs

Finally, I just want to give some love for our older dogs, who may be struggling with the very annoying puppy! Aura has found this week hard, because she is so sweet that she hates telling off the puppy. Even when he is jumping in her face. This makes her stressed and miserable. I've spent some time focusing on just her today, practising our agility moves, making a fuss of her and taking her away from the puppy, but with me. All of which have improved her mood no end.

It's hard to know what age is ideal when introducing a second dog. Too young and they can become very focused on each other, which can make them harder to manage. Too old and they can feel miserable and neglected. Being aware of the issues helps, of course.

Weekly Focus Challenge

Call your puppy! Say 'Name, come!' in the same excited way. Practice keeping it consistent. Do NOT just say their name over and over again. Give them a chance to respond. If you had someone just repeating your name over and over again, you wouldn't rush to respond. So try and stay calm and clear. When they get to you, say 'Yes!' and give them a treat. Then wait for them to wander off and do it again.

Do this at least 5 times per day.

Share a picture of your puppy gazing at you whilst sitting at your feet. Or of them coming after you have called them. Write about how you got on with the challenge below.

WEEK 2: PLAY WITH YOUR PUPPY - TRAINING

The importance of play

I'm pretty old, so I remember a time when 'playing' with your dog wasn't really something you did. We might have thrown sticks for our dogs on walks or in the garden. Not that we really walked our dogs that much. We certainly didn't train them!

Likewise, dogs played with each other if they lived together, or met on a walk. They might have got into a fight, but that wasn't that big a deal. Even 30 years ago, a family dog would regularly get into scraps with other dogs, but it wasn't considered a crime.

How far we have come! Nowadays, we value our dogs so much more. Well we pay a lot more for them to start with! We expect them to be a beloved family member and we don't want them being beaten up by other dogs when we are out. Unfortunately, whilst our expectations for our dogs have changed massively, our ability to manage them hasn't quite kept up.

Engaging with your dog

We are starting to appreciate that in order to manage our dog, we need to engage with him. I first learnt about 'play' with my dog only a few years ago. When doing agility, I have always been taught to reward their training, usually by throwing a toy. Some dogs don't really respond to this as a reward and need to have a treat instead.

I have gradually learnt that the best way to reward your dog is to teach them to properly play with you. This means getting a toy and playing 'tug' with you. Watching my puppies, I have discovered that they naturally do this. It is clearly a way to get the best bits of food. It's rather grisly, but puppies will fight over entrails and when you watch them with a toy you can see this behaviour.

What this play does is make your puppy think you are fun. This is the key. They then know that you are the source of happiness! Fantastic! Your puppy will then know that coming to you is a great idea. This is how you get the best and quickest recall.

Reward the recall

It's not quite enough to play with your puppy. You also need to provide tasty treats. Call them, reward, then play. Play, then call them and reward. I have noticed that if I want Quin to give up the toy, I need to let go, then call and reward with a treat. He will usually drop the toy to take the food.

Remember to wait! You need to be patient. It takes time for puppies to process the instructions. Don't always expect instant reactions. DO NOT keep on calling! Don't call their name repeatedly. If you keep saying their name, it just becomes white noise. Blah blah blah.

"Quin come." Wait. Here he comes. Hands together between your legs. Bring your hands up so he sits. Say "YES!" nice and clearly. Give a treat. Well, a bit of a treat.

Train when hungry

My top tip for training your puppy: make sure he is hungry. Don't try and train him straight after his meal. Equally, don't train him when he is tired.

Play with other dogs

This brings me to another key point: play with other dogs. I don't do much training when I have more than one puppy, because they are just too busy and too focused on each other. It's lovely to see dogs playing happily, but it does need managing. If you have a young dog (1-3 years old) and a puppy, chances are they will play all day! That's lovely, but you won't get much concentration from the puppy unless you keep them apart for some of the time.

DO NOT assume that your puppy MUST play with every other dog they see! On the contrary, teach your puppy that YOU are the most exciting thing on the walk. I'll talk about that more in my next post..

Weekly Focus Challenge

Play with your puppy. Try engaging him with a toy, playing a game of tug? Watch out for your fingers! A few minutes of play, then give him a treat and some praise. Then a bit more play. Do this every day. Ideally after they have come to you. Reward the recall, then play!

Share a picture of your puppy playing with you. Write about how you got on with the challenge below.

_____

_____

_____

_____

_____

_____

WEEK 3: BITING PUPPY? - PROBLEM

Puppy biting is such a problem, isn't it?

Puppies have VERY sharp teeth – everyone knows that! When they first arrive home at 8 weeks of age, they can be really bitey. Children soon go off their cute, fluffy puppy when they nip at ankles and chews fingers.

I see so much about people being exasperated with their puppies biting so much. Now I have a confession to make: I have never been bothered by a biting puppy! I've been pondering about why this might be and have come up with a few reasons.

Coping with biting:

1. Don't let your puppy become overtired. My puppies have a pretty calm life. I do play with them and I do make sure I spend some time every day training them. Apart from that, nothing much happens in our house. Even when my sons were small, we were not a household full of shouting and running around. It's hardly ever hectic. So my puppies don't get to that 'overtired' stage, where they just don't know what to do with themselves. That's when they can't control their biting and it gets much more frequent and harder!

2. Tell your puppy that it hurts! When puppies play with each other, or with adult dogs, they do occasionally hurt each other. You always hear a yelp when this happens. They then stop playing and look at each other. Then the play starts up again. So when a puppy accidentally bites me too hard, I yelp. Or at least, I say 'Ow!' Well that seems reasonable, doesn't it?

3. Let them know it is not acceptable. If my puppies are behaving in a way that is annoying, I say 'No!' and then call them away. I might even give them a tap on their nose if they are really getting carried away. Or just push them off and leave them alone for a minute. Again, this is the same way the adult dogs behave. Puppies are quick to learn.

Teething

Of course puppies do need to chew and bite, especially when they start to lose their baby teeth and replace them with adult teeth. Again, I've never particularly found this difficult. My top tip:

provide plenty of things to chew! Frozen carrot sticks are supposed to be good. Or food put into a frozen 'Kong'.

We don't give our dogs bones or sticks these days, because there is a risk of choking. (That doesn't mean they won't eat sticks from the garden if they can!)

Give it up!

I've noticed that Quin is very good at finding things in the garden that he then doesn't want to give up. He will run away from me if I try to take it from him.

DON'T CHASE HIM! He'll love that game! I have to call him, standing still, with a treat in my hand. If he thinks what he has is particularly fantastic, I might need an extra tasty treat – a bit of cheese. I offer him the treat and make sure I am being positive and exciting. He drops the bit of mud/hair/stick and comes to see me. I then slide round him to pick up the discarded yuck. Nice!

It's worth remembering to limit access to the garden at this age. It's a whole world out there, full of mischief to make! Holes to be dug, plants to be chewed, poo to be eaten. Of course it's tempting to leave the door open, so that he can go to the toilet when he needs to, but it's just not worth it.

Toileting – getting there

Trying to cover one topic per week is difficult at this age – there is so much to deal with! Quin is being really good with his toileting, on the whole. When he wakes up, I take him out and then give him loads of praise for going. I also have to remember to do this after he's been playing for a while. And after he's eaten of course. But the good news is that he can hold on for a while. He isn't going to the toilet indoors most of the time, with just an occasional accident (not usually on my watch :p)

Finally..

A quick training update – we have been practising our 'down' command. Every day, a few times. Then a few more times. I start by bringing him down with my hand, holding a treat. Then I try using the hand action without a treat, then giving the treat once he is down. You need to start without really saying anything, then add the word 'down'. Say it in the same voice every time, if you can.

The final stage is to give the command and wait. Don't move! See if he knows what you're on about. If not, use your hand. Then try again. If he isn't getting it, move him a bit and try again.

Weekly Focus Challenge

When and why is your puppy is biting you or other family members? Monitor times it occurs and think about how you could reduce this. Make a note of when he is sleeping more and make sure he is getting plenty of sleep in a quiet, secure space.

Share a picture of your puppy when he is calm. Write about how you got on with the challenge below.

WEEK 4: FIRST WALK - INFORMATION

First time out for a walk!

It's a day you look forward to, but also secretly dread. How will your puppy behave when they go out into the world? What will happen? Will you be able to manage?

Quin is my 8th puppy. I remember taking one puppy out for their first time on lead, 35 years ago and being amazed at how they danced around and dangled on the end of the lead! Coping with the lead is very much the first battle. Nowadays I make sure that puppies have met their collar and lead well before their first walk.

Vaccination restrictions

As a breeder, I don't vaccinate my puppies before they go to their new homes. This is because each veterinary practice has a different brand of vaccine and a different regime for giving these. My vet gives the first vaccine at 8 weeks and the second one three weeks later. The puppy can go out straight away after this, although not swimming in lakes and rivers for another month.

 Please make sure you follow the guidance given by your vet and respect their regime.

Going out out

Just because the puppy can't go out for a walk, does not mean they cannot go out! Of course I have taken them out for microchipping, hearing and eye tests and their school visits! Then they travel to their new home.

I hope that my puppy owners have taken their puppies out for visits to friends' houses. Or carried them along to meet people at the school gates. They might even go out for a walk in a puppy sling. (I can't do that with Quin – he's too heavy already :p). Finally though, the day is here and they are ready to go out out.

Off lead – surely not?

I ask my potential puppy owners when they should let their puppy off lead. Sometimes people say 'Six months?' A six month old puppy is fully grown. They can run – fast! Even a small toy breed can shoot across the ground at that age. So you've got absolutely no chance of catching them.

When you first take your dog out, you are their whole world! You are their comfort blanket, their familiar, loving, caring food provider. You should also be their fun playmate. If you really don't believe they will come back to you – get a longline. Then you can let them wander away from you, but still have some control. You can gently tug the line as you call them. If all else fails, you can hang onto the end and go and get them.

You shouldn't need to do that though. If you have done the practice recall around the house and garden, and played with them, you should be able to go for it!

How long should first walks be?

When you take your puppy out for their first walk, 15 minutes is long enough. It's an intense experience for a dog. There are so many smells! So much to look at! All that noise! Added to which you are making them think about coming back to you.

Do not imagine you need to 'tire out' a puppy. They will play all day long, unless they are asleep! Puppies are extremely active, but also sleep for long stretches. They must be able to regulate this activity level themselves. Enforced activity can do untold damage to joints. Not to mention the more you force a dog to exercise, the fitter they will get.

You wouldn't take a 2 year old child on a 3 mile run, would you? Well don't do it to a puppy either :(. Keep it short and sweet. A positive experience for you all. Then do it again tomorrow.

Weekly Focus Challenge

Take your puppy out for their first walk! How did it go? Were you brave enough to go for it and let them off? Did you manage to practise a recall? Did the puppy cope with being on the lead? Did you remember to take plenty of rewards?

Share a picture of your puppy on their first walk. Write about how you got on with the challenge below.

WEEK 5: SOCIALISATION - TRAINING

How do you socialise?

When you meet someone, do you rush up to them shouting 'Play with me'? Do you insist that everyone you meet talks to you and gives you a hug? Or do you calmly walk up and look at the person to see if they are interested in talking? Let's think about how dogs need to learn to say hello?

If your small dog runs up to my tiny puppy and chases them, do you think 'how sweet they're playing'? I don't think that. My puppy is frightened. He doesn't know your dog, so why would he want to play with them?

What will happen when Quin grows into a big dog (the size of a lab) and your dog runs up to him and chases him? He might turn round and say 'go away' and snap his teeth, which might catch your dog and draw blood. Who's fault will this be? *You* taught him that dogs are scary and rude.

Call your dog. Get them under control. Walk calmly towards me and say hello to me. If I stop to chat, your dog and mine will say hello. They might even play! I teach my dogs to ignore everything they pass, as a starting point. But if I say hello to someone, they can say hello. Calmly. It's not that I'm an anti-social person who never talks to anyone. It's that I want a calm, relaxing walk, with no stress, shouting or running away. No barking or lunging. No pulling on the lead. No lying down until other dogs go past and then leaping at them (I *really* hate that).

How to socialise your dog

Teach them to be calm and focus on you. Other dogs just aren't that interesting. There is no need to panic and run away. Nor is there any need to bark or lunge. This other dog is not a playmate, I am exciting and will play with you! One of the crucial parts of this process is how I behave with my dog. I MUST stay calm and positive. If I am nervous, particularly if my dog is on lead, my dog will know straight away and that will impact on how he reacts.

The next step

When you are confident that your dog is calm and feeling happy, you can try a bit of greeting. When I did this with Quin, he was not that confident. He thinks about running away, but is reassured by me standing calmly. He then comes through my legs, so nice and close to me. He enjoys saying hello. So much in fact he jumps up! He nearly gets rewarded for that, but fortunately he remembers he's not supposed to do that so is rewarded for sitting down.

Quin doesn't really want to engage with the other dog. It would like to sniff him, but it is on lead, so can't get there without pulling. Because he's pulling, he can't reach Quin and Quin isn't interested in talking to him (perhaps because he is pulling?) So then we calmly walk away.

What is socialisation? Why do we need it?

What is the ultimate goal here? I am aiming to teach my dogs to calmly pass other dogs on their walks. But I also want to be able to have them walk alongside other dogs, if I meet up with friends.

If you only have one dog, these issues are bigger and more difficult to overcome. If you have a breed of dog (or a mix of breeds) that are not particularly confident, such as a poodle, or a toy dog, you will find these issues more challenging to train.

Border Collies want to learn and to please. Research has shown that they are more intelligent than other breeds and will pick up training more quickly. But of course you can train other breeds. It just takes time, effort and maybe some professional help from a good dog trainer. NB: Border Collies pick up bad habits *really* quickly!

Other training progress

I've started teaching Quin to 'wait'. This takes a long time, but is an essential command, one that I use every day. I will be adding time, distance and distraction over the next few months. Finally, I am very pleased with his on-lead walking. I don't walk him on lead very much, but is vital that he is able to do so.

Weekly Focus Challenge

How are you going to react when you see other dogs whilst you are out? Make yourself stay calm. Try to get your puppy's attention and give them lots of treats whilst people go past, then play! Be interesting, rewarding and exciting. Think about what you are enjoying with your puppy's walks? What still needs working on?

Share a picture of your puppy out and about. Write about how you got on with the challenge below.

WEEK 6: JUMPING UP - PROBLEM

Don't jump up!

A dog that jumps up at people is annoying. Fact. People rarely like it. Unless of course it is *their* dog, when they might actively encourage it. Which is a bit of a shame, because it makes training a lot more difficult. If you are out walking your dog though, chances are you do NOT want them rushing up to strangers and leaping into their faces. So why do they do that? And what can we do about it?

Why dogs jump up

With this litter, my tenth, I finally realised why dogs jump up. When they were just a few weeks old, the mum is not with them all the time. She arrives into the den or run and they rush to greet her. Initially this is just for milk. They scrabble around to get onto a teat and when they are too big to fit lying down, she will stand so they can get into position underneath her.

A few weeks later, they have started to eat solid food. In the wild, this consists of her regurgitating food for them. The puppies all rush to her mouth and 'kiss' her, licking and pawing at her.

Steps to stop jumping up

It is perfectly possible to stop your puppy from jumping up at you. But it takes CONSISTENCY and you must be **PERSISTENT**. Here are the steps:

1. Sit down with all members of your household and agree that this is a behaviour you want to stop. You can have plenty of cuddles with your dog, without letting them jump up when they see you.
2. When you come into the room with your puppy, DO NOT give attention if they jump up at you. Say nothing. No eye contact.
3. If they persist in jumping, turn away from them. Walk away from them, ignoring them completely.
4. When they stop jumping up, bend down and give lots of praise and fuss. Ideally, say 'yes!' as you do this. You are rewarding the correct behaviour. Great.
5. Model this behaviour for your family and friends. Ask them to copy you.

Out on walks

Ideally, you then need to continue this good practice when you are out and about. You should initially stop your puppy from greeting people on walks. Call your dog to you and reward their attention. Then when they are calm and still, the person you meet can bend down and make a fuss of them. Perfect!

What is rewarding?

There are various things that your dog finds rewarding:

- Praise – your dog loves you and anything you say in a positive voice is rewarding to them
- Patting – a gentle fuss around their head or ears is tremendously rewarding
- Play – activity with a toy is great fun!
- Food – (can't think of a way to say food beginning with p). Of course food is a great reward. Tiny amounts though.

If you push your dog off you when they jump up, you are rewarding your dog with 'patting'. If you shout at it, you are rewarding it with 'praise' by speaking to it. Have a look at my 'fun quiz' for more ideas about how *not* to reward your dog…

Managing visitors to your house

Of course not everyone you know will understand the importance of good dog behaviour and they may be really pleased to meet your dogs. But some visitors may be quite nervous around dogs and definitely don't want to be leapt on!

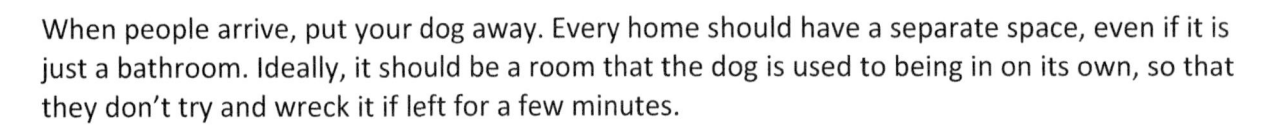

When people arrive, put your dog away. Every home should have a separate space, even if it is just a bathroom. Ideally, it should be a room that the dog is used to being in on its own, so that they don't try and wreck it if left for a few minutes.

Greet your guests, bring them in. Ideally, you want to get them seated and settled before you bring the dogs in. Then calmly let the puppy in. If people are sitting down there is less chance of them being jumped on and it is easier for the visitor to bend down to stroke them. If the puppy jumps up, try calling them away. Calm them down, then let them try again. If they get too excited, take them away. Do this by calling them, not dragging them. Put them away again, preferably with a treat.

Remember, good manners cost nothing – just a bit of time and effort.

Weekly Focus Challenge

How are you going to stop your puppy from jumping up? Be aware of your behaviour when you come into the house. Talk to family and friends about what you plan to do to stop the jumping up and why that is important to you. Reward your puppy for not jumping up.

Share a picture of your puppy sitting calmly at your feet. Write about how you got on with the challenge below.

WEEK 7: TRAVELLING - INFORMATION

Puppy travelling – how can you get them used to the car?

This post is about putting your dog in the car, not about going on holiday, or travelling abroad. One day we will do those things, but not today…

Like so many things in life, getting a puppy used to travelling by car takes practice. It's as simple as that. Lots of dogs do not like going in the car to start with. When I take my puppies to the vet's for their microchips, or to the specialist vet's for their hearing and eye tests, they often cry for most of the journey. Usually some of them are sick.

When they go off to their new homes they must travel in a crate, in the boot, or on a harness on the seat. They are very often frightened and stressed. Even covering the crate doesn't necessarily help. Earplugs might be needed!

Travelling in crates

Dogs must be secure when travelling in cars – it is a legal requirement. The most common way of achieving this is by having a dog guard fitted between the back seat and the boot area. The advantage of this is that it is inexpensive and easy to fit or remove. It should not impact the sale of your car in the future (although the mud and dog hair might!)

However, if you are planning on leaving your dog in your car, where they might chew, you might be better off getting a crate to go into the boot. This can be a free-standing crate that just sits in the boot (see above), or it could be a structure that is specially fitted. When you have multiple dogs, people normally find that a van is the best option.

One of the key advantages of this option if you plan to go to any events or shows with your dog is that the dogs can be safely left inside the cage, with the car boot or doors open. It's also brilliant if you are taking the dogs away with you, as they have plenty of room.

Other travel options

Some people don't like using crates, or they don't feel they have space in their car. You can use a harness to keep the dog secure on the back seat. Personally I feel that a dog is likely to chew through a harness. I also feel that a crate gives a dog more opportunity to change position and stand up, if they want to. You can also put a water bowl in a crate.

How can we help?

As I've said, the main thing in getting a dog used to travelling is to take your dog out and about. Don't make the only time they are in the car be when they go to the vet! Take them out for short journeys to different walks. This has the advantage of being a really positive experience for your dog. It also gives you the chance of a change of scenery.

I tend to walk from home for only around half my walks. The rest of the time I go off to woods or fields. I park in places where my dogs can go straight out from the van, with no lead walking at all. Lovely!

If your dog is really stressed by the car, try feeding them in the boot, with the engine off. If that is too stressful, start with giving treats next to the car. Gradually increase the time in the car. Turn the engine on and sit quietly, with the dog in their crate. Then start to go for short journeys, without stopping or getting out.

Quin's other news

Walking around other dogs continues to be a challenge. The other day I had two dogs, including a greyhound, run over to us, causing Quin to run away from me. The owner called them, but it was a bit of a challenge and I had to go and fetch Quin from where he had run to hide under the van.

Fortunately, some dogs are polite and don't rush at us. Quin is happy to sit by me whilst they go past, or even cope while they sniff him. We have managed to walk alongside a few other dogs, which is great.

This morning someone remarked "What a well behaved puppy!" That's lovely, but really, I'm not doing much. It's a slow, steady process. Keeping on doing it, every day. We do a few recalls, a bit of a wait. On lead, off lead (mainly off lead). Playing with my puppy. Engaging with him. He's a happy boy, loving his life. Which reminds me to go and check what he's eating..

Weekly Focus Challenge

Take your puppy out regularly in the car. Make sure they are secure. Reward them for getting themself into the into the car. Go on short journeys every day, preferably with a positive experience at the end of the trip. Watch out for your puppy jumping out of the car, as this may stress their joints unnecessarily.

Share a picture of your puppy in your car. Write about how you got on with the challenge below.

WEEK 8: PLAYDATE! - TRAINING

Socialisation – part 2: meeting a friend

This post is really about recall, but it's also about socialisation. On my post two weeks ago about socialisation, I talked about training your dog to ignore other dogs, to be calm and not lunge or bark. I wanted to be able to stay relaxed and calm as other dogs walk past.

But life would be pretty boring if we never talked to anyone else! I definitely like seeing friends and I love walking my dogs with other people. So how would Quin react to meeting up with another puppy his age? And would he ever come back to me?

Meeting another dog

This morning I met up with a friend, who has a five-and-a-half-month-old Border Collie puppy. We had both pups on lead to start with and managed the distance between them and the way they said hello. It was interesting, because Quin immediately knew the puppy was a friend. He recognised his breed and the age of the other dog, not surprisingly. His behaviour was far more confident and he straight away asked if Isla would play with him.

When dogs meet, they ask to play with a 'play bow'. This means 'Hello, I'm friendly. I would like to play with you'. Your dog will do this to you, but you might not realise. Obviously they know you, so to you they are saying 'you are my family and I love you. Now give me food/walk/play!' It's their way of saying 'please'.

Off they go!

When we got to the field, we immediately let the puppies off lead. They can't play together if they are on lead. It was so lovely to see that they ran around together straight away. They roared about, up and down, probably going a bit further than Quin would go from me. Then they stopped. After just a few minutes they had a pause. Take a breath, then go! That is the ideal point to do a quick recall, to get them to check in with you.

Recall away from distractions

It's very exciting, being around another dog! So much fun, being chased and chasing. So don't expect a miracle? I bet if you call your other half, they aren't there in a second, are they? What about your children, do they respond immediately when you call them? And if someone calls you and you are busy on your phone, do you say 'Coming!' but actually take a while to actually go?

Get a grip. Your puppy will not come back to you straight away. But IF you have done your training, practising that recall again and again, you will find that they DO come back to you, even when they are playing. Well, they will in a minute...

Always reward

Don't forget the reward. YOU MUST REWARD EVERY TIME! And be pleased to see them, even if it has taken longer than normal. Have good, tasty rewards. Grab their collar and stroke their neck and ears. Use a toy to engage them if you can.

Don't keep calling

If you say your dog's name, over and over again, it just becomes white noise. Blah, blah, blah. Boring. So try to just say clearly 'Quin come'. Wait. Then wait a bit longer. Of course in a really distracting situation like this, it's incredibly difficult not to keep on saying his name. Panic sets in! But patience is rewarded.

When we were out I called him and he turned to come. Then Isla ran past him and he decided that was much more fun. But he did turn towards me and then did come over. I get his attention with an 'Oi!' rather than repeatedly calling. I laugh, because I am being realistic about how hard this is for him. He comes. I am thrilled! I am hopeless, but it is my first time with such a BIG distraction!

Manage it

Don't overdo, especially when they are still so young. We were out for around 20 minutes. They were off lead for around half that time. That's it, it was enough to tire them out. And I wouldn't want to do that every day. Now and again is fine. Lovely to have friends though.

Weekly Focus Challenge

Arrange to go for a walk with a friend, preferably with a young dog. Hold your breath, then let them off lead. I know it's a challenge, but it will be fine. Let them play and give them space. Then call them back. Be exciting! DO NOT keep on saying their name. If they ignore you, give it a minute, breathe, then try again. If they really don't want to come, run away, preferably squeaking a toy and calling in a positive, high-pitched voice! Then make sure you let them go again. It's fine. What do you think your puppy gained from this experience?

Share a picture of your puppy on their walk. Write about how you got on with the challenge below.

WEEK 9: TOILETING – PROBLEM

How to house train your puppy

I've left this to week 9 to talk about because although you need to get started in week 1, you will probably find by week 9 you are getting sick of clearing up the puddles! It's not too late, you will get on top of it. Don't despair!

Puppies are babies

I recently received an enquiry recently asking me if the puppies I produce are sent to their new homes fully toilet trained. Er, no. At 8 weeks of age, puppies are still babies and do not have full bladder control.

Over the years, as I have had litters of puppies and watched them grow, I have realised that they will try and toilet away from their bed almost before they can walk. Their mother cleans them up completely for the first few weeks and you rarely see any mess in that time. Then they stagger and stumble away from where they are feeding, feeling a different texture underfoot and toileting there.

As they grow, puppies become weeing and pooing monsters! It's one of the hardest parts of having a litter of puppies in your home – it's a constant mess. Once they are up and about, they will toilet anywhere. I have newspaper in the run, which I change regularly. Other people use different materials. Many puppies are kept on sawdust or straw, in outside runs, or sheds, simply to help manage the mess.

Dogs don't care

Dogs do have very different toileting behaviours to us. Because they are ruled by their noses, they use their urine to scent, or mark where they have been. They also urinate on top of where other dogs have been. Once one dog has urinated in one place, every other dog in the world will want to go there! So if you have a male dog who marks something, you must expect every other male to also add their scent. Beware cleaning with normal household cleaners – they are likely to make the problem worse, as the ammonia just smells like wee to a dog! And they can still smell traces of wee for years – trust me!

Dogs will also poo in particular places. My dogs do toilet in the garden, which I clear every day. I know that each dog has one or two places they go, every day. So they do care where they go. But they don't care what you think about where they go! In other words, in makes no real difference to them if it is inside or outside, on a walk or in the garden.

Dogs won't go to the toilet in their bed, if they can help it. But a bit of wee doesn't really bother them and they will happily lie in it if they have to. They also eat poo! The Kennel Club recently produced this great article: Why does my dog eat poo? We might find it disgusting, but for them, it's no big deal.

Getting started

I think understanding toileting from a dog's point of view does help us to manage their behaviour. As I've said, I know that dogs move off their bed (usually) to toilet from a very young age and I do try to keep their run clean.

When they are up and about, I ensure they can go outside as soon as possible. They have access to grass, which they much prefer to poo on. I also start to take them all outside to wee as soon as they wake up, or after they have eaten, or after they have been playing… I call them, "Puppy, puppy, puppy" and they all come running! Of course I can't do that all day every day; six week old puppies are particularly trying!

HOW TO TOILET TRAIN YOUR PUPPY

When they go off to their new homes, this is how you get started – every hour, after a sleep, after food, after play, go out with them. Go onto the grass and say "Do you want a wee?" Or "Be quick!" or "Be clean". It's up to you what you say, but then as soon as they have toileted, **REWARD!**

That's it. Keep doing this until they go outside, not inside.

Reward every time

It's really about consistency. *The more effort you make, the less 'accidents' you will have to clear up.* If you can't be bothered to be with your puppy and pay attention to its behaviour, you can expect to step in the odd wee!

Naturally we can't be with our dogs every second of every day. When we get a puppy at 8 weeks of age, they will need to toilet at least every hour during the day. They can't go through the night without needing to toilet.

They poo four times or more. For me, I prefer to give my dogs space to toilet, in a run either outside or inside.

Dry at night

Puppies can usually last all night from around ten weeks of age. They can then go into a crate, to stop them rampaging, playing and chewing all night long! Crates are a great way of helping them to learn bladder control and managing when and where they do toilet. You may still have accidents in the crate, if you leave them in there too long, or if they get an upset tummy. Border Collies are a breed that are prone to sensitive digestion, so you need to feed them something consistently.

Keep going

If you get your puppy in the summer, it's tempting to just leave the door open and let them find their way outside. Dogs prefer to toilet on a soft surface, so if you don't have any rugs or mats, they should go outside. However, if you do that, your puppy might then be confused when it gets colder and you shut the door! So you might then be back to square one. Go out with them, wait for them to go. **REWARD!**

NB: *If they find the garden too exciting and rush around playing and exploring, you need to put them on a lead and just stand with them and wait.*

Of course they might not always want to go when you want to take them. This is when is good if you can be around your puppy for a while. If they are wandering around a bit restlessly, that is probably what they want. Some puppies are kind enough to stand by the door and wait for you to open it, but they won't wait for long! You can teach them to ring a bell on the door, with time and patience. Be careful though, or your dog will have you at their beck and call, ringing every five minutes just to go into the garden and play!

Should you tell them off?

In the old days (a *very* long time ago) we used to show our dogs their wee or poo and shout at them (I won't mention rubbing their noses in it). Thankfully we don't do that any more. But it's not unreasonable to say 'NO!' sharply if you catch your dog in the act of toileting in the house. They can understand when you're not happy, it just needs to be *very* clear what it is for.

Above all, praise them for toileting in the right place. If you keep going, patiently and consistently, you'll get there in the end. I'm writing this post when Quin is over four months old. He's pretty good, on the whole. We caught him digging a hole in the lawn the other day and got cross, so he came in the house and weed everywhere. Silly us! And he tends to leak a bit if we don't let him out when he needs to go.

Excited wees

When you greet a puppy, they wee. They just can't help being excited and they don't have enough control. This usually sorts itself out by the time they are six months old. You can help by being less exciting, or by letting them out before you greet people. Or by saying hello to them outside, when it doesn't matter so much. Toilet training your puppy is a challenge. Like everything else relating to your dog, it requires effort, patience and persistence. Oh and don't forget the **REWARDS**!

Weekly Focus Challenge

All day long, take your puppy outside, wait for them to toilet and reward them for going. Go out with them, even if it's the middle of the night or it's cold and raining. Watch them. Wait for them. Give them a verbal prompt, before and after. Again and again. And again. It's hard work and takes effort. The more you do it, the better they will be. If you can't be bothered, they won't be bothered. You can't tell them off for your lack of effort. NB: If they start playing in the garden, you will have to put them on lead to help manage their behaviour. You cannot leave them unsupervised and expect them to perform. Or not come back into the house and toilet.

Share a picture of your puppy being good. Write about how you got on with the challenge below.

WEEK 10: DOG TOYS - INFORMATION

What's the point of dog toys?

Why do we buy toys for our dogs? What are they for? Like most people, I love a bit of retail therapy every now and again. I am seduced by cute, furry toys, with funny faces. I love buying presents for my dogs. They love receiving presents from me! They are so happy to have a new toy, running around waving it about and making sure to give it a good shake, or a squeak.

I suppose one of the reasons for buying toys is that it gives us and our dogs pleasure. They enjoy the stimulation of having something different to play with.

Destructor puppy!

The trouble with buying cute cuddly toys for your dog is that they don't last long! Puppies have sharp teeth and they absolutely LOVE ripping toys to shreds. They scatter the stuffing all round the room and eat ears, feet and hands, which then end up littering the garden when they reappear. Oh dear!

The thing is, if you don't give your puppy toys to play with, they will find other things to chew and destroy! That's what a puppy does best. So far we have lost a phone cable and a cushion to our darling Quin, but I know there is more to come, because this morning we found a tooth.

Teething trouble

At around 4-5 months of age, puppies lose their baby teeth and their adult teeth come through. Just like with human babies, that is annoying and painful for puppies. They find relief through chewing.

In the wild, they would chew sticks and roots, or probably bits of fur and skin from the animals killed by their mother. You can buy bits of animals for your puppy to chew, such as chicken feet or pigs ears. Beware antlers though, as these can break teeth, leading to expensive vet bills for dentistry work. Luna lost a canine to an antler. Teething puppies can also be soothed with food, such as frozen Kongs, carrots or ice cubes.

Different toys for different tasks

When shopping for your dog, you need to think about meeting a variety of needs. Soft toys are great for playing with, squeaking and believe it or not, cuddling! My dogs definitely love their soft toys and some last for ages. Others, not so much.

Dogs definitely need hard toys to chew. These are often bone, or stick shaped and made of plastic, rubber or nylon. Beware rawhide, as these have been shown to be produced using hideous chemical processes, which are bad for our dogs. They also cause blockages.

Balls are of course essential. Most dogs love chasing after a ball. My dogs have a box of tennis balls they have discovered on walks; Aura is the queen of the ball. They have so much fun running around after a ball, giving it to one another – they hardly need my input at all!

A word of caution about ball chuckers: I used to use one to give the dogs long, fast runs, but decided that it was just too problematic. Too much running at top speed and jumping for a ball leads to early onset arthritis, joint damage and other possible injuries. It is also too stimulating, which can just make your dog hyper, rather than tiring them out, as you probably intended. Oh and chewing tennis balls has now been shown to erode teeth, so again, this needs to be managed.

Tuggy toys are another must have for many dogs. I use tuggy play to engage with my dog and keep their focus on me whilst training. It is super rewarding and really helps stop my puppy reacting to things going past him whilst on walks. At agility, it's a great way of stopping dogs getting wound up by other dogs training, or competing. Some people think tuggy play can be too distracting for dogs and lead to undesired behaviour, so again, this needs to be kept in context. Dogs will play tuggy with each other, which can be fun, as long as it doesn't lead to fights.

Alternatives to toys

If you don't have endless funds to spend on buying toys, there are alternatives. Soft toys can be made from old socks for example. A pair of socks, one inside the other, filled with the stuffing and squeaker from an old toy can provide plenty of fun. Or buy soft toys from a charity shop.

You can use yogurt pots, juice or water bottles, or flower pots for dogs to chase around and chew. If you fill a bottle with gravel that provides an extra level of sensory play. Watch the chewing of this plastic though and take it away once it starts to break up as the pieces are much sharper than plastic bones.

Tuggy toys can be made from bits of vet bed, cut into strips. Or how about getting an old pair of jeans, tearing it into strips and plaiting it? My puppies love playing with these and they last a good while.

Toy management

As you have seen, most toys have limitations. They need managing and you need to be aware of what your dog is doing, as much as possible. But they are safer than chewing sticks or stones. Ultimately, it is about keeping your dog occupied in a manageable way, rather than letting them destroy your home. There are now plenty of toys available to help challenge your dog, such as licky mats, snuffle mats etc.

When they are teething, people often despair and think about re-homing. Like many stages of puppyhood, this will pass. Most dogs stop chewing, most of the time.

Weekly Focus Challenge

Provide a variety of toys for your puppy. Monitor their play and make sure they are not eating things they are not supposed to! This is harder than it sounds and you will definitely have a few inappropriate toys chewed.

Share a picture of your puppy with a favourite toy. Write about how you got on with the challenge below.

WEEK 11: WAIT! - TRAINING

Teaching your puppy to wait

Do we really need to teach this to our dogs? This is by far the most important command to teach a dog, in my opinion. It is the lesson I want my puppy to learn as soon as possible, but it is pretty tricky to teach! Again, this is something I started from day one with Quin, but it takes ages to teach, so I'm focusing on it now.

Why wait? What do I use it for?

- Stopping my dog from heading into danger
- Stopping my dog from approaching another dog
- Waiting to cross a road
- Stopping them from rushing at their food
- Stopping them pushing past me through a door (rude)
- Making them wait when I open the door to the garden, or to go into the van
- Enabling me to take nice pictures of my dog(s)
- Waiting on the start line in agility

I'm sure you will find other uses for a good solid wait. It is absolutely invaluable. It is useful but also keeps them safe.

How do you start?

Call your dog to you. Have them sitting at your feet. Give them a treat for coming. Then get eye contact with them. Say 'wait'. I usually put up my hand, or my finger to reinforce. Wait a few seconds. Say 'yes!' and reward.

Do this a few (hundred) times. The amount of times you need to do each stage and the speed with which you can move forward depends on:
- Your dog
- Your consistency
- Your patience

Not all dogs are as quick to learn and keen to please as Border Collies. So this can be challenging. But it is worth the effort.

Next step

Once you have your dog able to sit and focus on you for a few seconds, you can start to move away. Take a step back. Stand sideways and wait. Then step back in and reward. From there you can gradually (very gradually) increase the distance and time.

It will go wrong! When you move off, your puppy will probably follow you. That's fine. Step back and put your puppy back into a sit. Say 'wait' again. Step away and wait. If you can move away and then step back in without movement from the puppy, you are succeeding. It might take a while!

You might find it easier to put the dog into a down to teach the wait. Get them into a down and reward. Then say wait and step away. I have found Quin is less fidgety and more relaxed in a down. He can be a bit watchful and anxious in a sit.

Moving on

Once you have a bit of distance and you feel that your dog understands the basic concept, you can start to make it more challenging. There are all sorts of ways you can do this. Here are some options:

- Increasing distance
- Turning your back
- Moving around
- Going round the back of the dog
- Moving quickly
- Waving your arms around
- Making a noise

- Having a toy

There is a lot you can do to challenge the wait! You can mix it up, sometimes just standing beside your dog, at other times moving around. It's a great idea to call your dog to you, from the wait. This is known as a 'formal recall', as the dog remains calm and still, then comes neatly to you and sits at your feet. It looks impressive! The hardest part of this is that your puppy will anticipate what you want and set off before you call them. So you need to go back to your dog for some of the time and reward the waiting, before you reward the recall.

Be realistic

If it goes wrong, that's fine. Put the dog back and start again. If you can't get the distance or movement, go back a step. Move away and be still. Or just stay by your dog until they are happy with the wait.

Don't push your luck. If you try to make your dog wait in a busy, distracting environment, you will find it hard. Try and practice where it is quiet. Or go somewhere busy, but wait beside your dog, building their confidence.

Advanced wait

As I've said, there is a great deal you can do to challenge the wait. I will talk about that in a few months' time. There is also a difference between 'wait' and 'stop', although you might use the same command for both.

Weekly Focus Challenge

Start working on your wait. Make sure you are realistic. Build it up slowly. Share a picture of your puppy waiting while you take a picture. How far away from them can you go?

Write about how you got on with the challenge below.

WEEK 12: BARKING AND HOWLING - PROBLEM

How to manage your dog's howling and barking

Dogs bark a lot don't they? It's one of the ways they communicate. We often find it annoying and sometimes frightening. It can be difficult to understand why a dog is making so much noise. Or it can be challenging to stop them. It is a complex issue, so I will only be able to touch on some of the key points here.

Excited barking

This is probably the most common reason why dogs bark. Something is happening! The doorbell has rung! A bird flew past! There's a cat in the garden! A squirrel ran along the fence! You got up! And so on. Your dog is communicating with you that something is happening they think you want to know about. Or they are just excited and reacting to that excitement.

How to react: DO NOT shout at your dog. Your dog will think you are also barking! Hurray! Let's all carry on barking. Lol. Call them, calmly and as quietly as you can. Get their attention away from the thing that is exciting and reward the quiet. Make sure they know that whatever it is, it's just not that interesting. The less reaction you give, the more likely they are to stop barking and generally reacting to the stimulus.

However, this is *very hard* for a dog to control. It's a base instinct, which means they react without thinking. Just as we shout at our dog for being annoying! Hmm. Another word of caution – if there are likely to be *lots* of things to bark at, try moving the dog to a different space, where there is less stimulation.

Or reduce access to windows, or the garden. It's a bit of a losing battle, if you have a constant stream of squirrels in the garden, to try and stop your dog barking at them.

Frightened barking

Again, this is an instinctive reaction to a stimulus, but this time it is about fear of the unknown. Who is that person? What are they doing here? I don't know this other dog? Why is there a loud noise? Quin barks at his reflection quite a bit at the moment, bless him. We just ignore that. Or call away and reassure him.

I'm sure you can tell the difference between excited and frightened barking? Excited barking will happen alongside a wriggling, waggy, smiley dog. Fearful barking will be accompanied by hackles up and backing off. Your dog will be tense and focused on the fearful object.

You might see both these types of barking at home and whilst you are out. Understanding the difference can help you react to them. If your dog is afraid, they need reassurance. So again, shouting at your dog to be shut up is NOT the solution. Once more, quiet reassurance and distraction is a better solution.

Just be careful that you don't reinforce the fearful response. Call away, distract, be calm. Then reward. Otherwise your dog is warning you that something might be frightening and then thinks you want them to tell you every time they see something similar. You are not saying 'thanks for telling me about that'! You are rewarding them for stopping.

Howling

When a dog howls, they are properly distressed. Or really, really excited! Again, you need to understand the circumstances and why the behaviour is happening, in order to react to it appropriately. Busy is my main howler. She howls when she is missing out on something. If someone goes off on a walk or out to training without her, she gives a really plaintive, sad little howl.

Howling is not nice to hear. Sometimes a dog howls briefly and then stops, realising that nothing is changing. Sadly, dogs who are left alone for long periods may continue to howl, or bark pitifully, which is horrible for neighbours.

Separation anxiety

If you get a puppy when you are around ALL the time, and then suddenly leave them alone, you will make your dog sad and anxious. This is a very real problem and one that is unfortunately becoming far more common following the pandemic. It is known as 'separation anxiety'.

The trick is to make sure your puppy knows that being alone is fine. The earlier and more often you do this, the better your dog will cope. I do not stay with my litters of puppies all day every day and nor do their mothers. They are safe and warm, so they just sleep, or play, until we return. When I keep a puppy from a litter, I leave them alone from day one. I put him to bed in a crate, at night. Or during the day, when I walk the other dogs. It's only for an hour or so during the day, but I go out little and often. Or I go into a different room (including the toilet!) and make sure that the puppy can't follow. Building confidence is the key to tackling this issue.

Distraction toys

I always make sure my dogs are safe and have things to chew, such as Kongs, if needed. You can also try giving a dog something to distract them, such as a 'Lickimat'. Whatever you do, as always with your dog, make sure you are ***patient, persistent and consistent.*** Your dog will thank you!

Weekly Focus Challenge

Think about when and why your dog is barking. Practice leaving them alone for longer periods, managing them so that they are safe. Reward them when they are calm and settled.

Share a picture of your puppy lying calmly. Write about how you got on with the challenge below.

WEEK 13: DOGs AND CHILDREN – INFORMATION

How do I manage my puppy with children around?

As they grow and change, our puppies have different needs and react in different ways to situations. Managing a puppy in a family home is not just about the week the puppy arrives. It is an ongoing challenge.

Biting puppy

I was recently asked advice about a puppy that was biting a lot and really hurting its family. I referred them to my early post about puppy biting. This can be an ongoing issue though and as their adult teeth come through, then can get a bit snappy, or just occasionally carried away when playing.

My top tip in managing your puppy's biting tendency is to stop them getting over-excited or carried away. Don't let them take advantage of you or think that it is OK to have them mouthing or biting you 'just because they are being playful'. It is never OK to allow this behaviour if you are not able to manage it. So if it starts to happen, move yourself or the puppy away from that situation.

Learning boundaries

Everyone needs to learn what is and is not acceptable in different situations. Children need to know how to manage themselves around their dog. You should NEVER trust your dog alone with your children when they are both young and inexperienced. I would always keep them apart unless they were supervised. Children sometimes struggle to know when enough is enough. Dogs have very sharp teeth. These two things do not mix well. NB: Learn your dog's calming signals?

In the olden days, (ie when I was a child), we understood the expression 'let sleeping dogs lie'. If a dog is asleep, leave them alone. Don't go over and poke your puppy, or pester them in any way. If you call them, you might get a response. When your dog is awake, they will play with you. But don't expect them to always be ready to play. Dogs spend most of every day asleep. Please respect that?

Teach play skills

Dogs and children love to play together, right? Well, yes, probably. But again, this needs to be managed. I have had to learn how to play effectively with my puppies, so it's not something that we understand instinctively.

I've talked a lot on my website about the way dogs play with each other. They love to play 'snap-snap' which gets quite lively and can sound aggressive. They also play chase, roaring around the furniture and jumping on and off things. Then dogs will also play tug with toys. This is the game Quin loves me to play with him. He brings me a toy and asks me to hold it so he can pull against me.

Sunny was the expert at explaining to people what she wanted them to do. Throw the ball! And again! Over and over again. Border Collies are relentless in this respect. Other dog breeds are not quite so persistent. Nor are they so good at explaining what they want. Some dogs like a bit of 'rough and tumble', but many dogs won't like this at all. Or they might get carried away and start to be a bit too aggressive.

Enough is enough

I can tell when my dogs have had enough when playing together. The sound changes – it is louder and sharper. Watch out for this – it means the game must end! A shout from me will bring things to an end, but for some people, dogs need to be separated before a proper fight starts.
Some dogs wind up other dogs, just as some children wind up other children. Quin likes to go and say hello to the other dogs if they've been apart. Aura doesn't like him doing this and grumbles noisily. I always say 'Quin, don't annoy Aura.' It's not her fault he is being annoying. So don't blame an older child if the younger one is being irritating? Equally, watch out for children winding up the dog – sometimes it's a fun game, but it could have fatal consequences.

There is plenty of advice about managing dogs and children, both on my website and elsewhere. As with everything dog-related, it requires a bit of thought and effort. Don't just expect it will be fine?

Weekly Focus Challenge

How is your dog around children? If you don't have any, try and visit family or friends so you can assess this interaction. Dogs can become very wary of children if they do not have this interaction. If you do have children, how easy is it to manage them around your dog? Do you supervise their play? Do you keep them separated when you are not around? Does your child understand the dog's rules for playing and not playing?

Share a picture of your dog and children. Write about how you got on with the challenge below.

_____

_____

_____

_____

_____

_____

WEEK 14: ON LEAD WALKING – TRAINING

Walking on lead

I am going to talk about generally walking on lead this week and will focus on specific problems with lead walking next week. I've just been reminded of the excellent Kennel Club Good Citizen Dog Scheme. Looking at the requirements for the different levels perfectly sums up what we need our dogs to do while they are on lead.

At the 'puppy' stage of this scheme, walking on lead requires the following:

Walking in a Controlled Manner

With the puppy on lead, and without distractions, the owner and puppy should walk for approximately 20 paces and include a turn. They should demonstrate that this can be done without undue inconvenience to themselves or others. A tight lead does not necessarily result in classification "Not Ready".

Quin is not perfect, far from it! But he is under control and relatively calm. That's fine for his age and experience level. I'm pretty happy with how he is generally.

What do you need from your dog?

I think before we talk about walking on lead, you need to think about what you want from your dog? Most of us want the following:

- to be able to clip the lead on easily
- to be able to walk along calmly with our dog beside us
- being able to stop or turn without having to yank or pull the dog
- crossing roads safely and calmly
- not having to walk too quickly, or too slowly.

In addition we ideally want to be able to go past obstacles and other people and dogs without a big reaction.

Go off lead

In my opinion, your dog should be able to go on lead for as short a time as possible, if at all. I feel like this because I have Border Collies. BCs are terrible on lead, even when they are highly trained in obedience. They are just too fast, too keen and too impatient! I remember going to an obedience show and seeing people being tanked around by their Border Collies – it was shocking!

As a result, I let my dogs off lead as soon as possible. Around half my walks involve a 5 minute drive to the woods, or fields. They go straight in the van, then out and away! For my other walks, they are on lead for 5 minutes through my housing estate and then away! To be absolutely honest, they are only lead so they don't poo in people's gardens. They don't pull my arms off, but 5 keen Border Collies don't walk slowly!

Lead or harness?

These days, we are thankfully much more aware of our dogs' welfare. We sadly haven't made the sale of prong collars illegal here yet (sign the petition please?) However, we are aware that even a normal collar and lead can cause discomfort and choking.

The trend is therefore to use a harness. However, these come in many different styles and don't always fit well. There is also an issue that some harnesses can restrict movement or cause discomfort in other ways.

Personally, I don't use a harness for a number of reasons:

- dogs in a harness are more inclined to lean into it and pull. This is fine for canicross, but not great for every day.
- harnesses are a right faff to put on and off. If you have more than one dog, who can be bothered?
- if a dog is off lead, why do they need a harness?

However, if you have one dog, who has to do a lot of on lead walking, then a harness is far better for your dog than a simple collar.

NB: if you do use a harness, remember that you MUST include a name tag. It is a legal requirement to have identification on your dog and you can be prosecuted if you do not have this. I use Indigo Dog Tags as they are easy to clip onto a flat lead, such as my beautiful Silverfoot Dog Collars (only the best for my dogs).

Extending leads

I understand why people use these, honestly I do. Extendable leads are great if you are too scared to let your dog off lead. You can let them wander about and sniff, but you can still hang onto the end if you need to. Again, I don't use these – I feel they are just an accident waiting to happen. The thin, nylon line is perfect for cutting into skin, getting caught around legs and causing a trip hazard. As with harnesses, you are really encouraging your dog to pull. The dog leans into the lead to extend it. A much better solution is a longline. These allow the dog to wander about, with no pulling required and a 'safety line' for you.

NB: Even a medium dog such as a Springer Spaniel or Border Collie is able to cause a fair amount of damage and/or pull you off your feet.

Walking on lead – conclusion

Teaching your dog to walk nicely on lead is a real challenge! There are a number of options to help you manage this. I'll talk about how to manage problem behaviour in the next post. The best solution is simply to let them off lead!

Weekly Focus Challenge

What is your dog like on lead? How much have you worked on this? What equipment do you use and could this be better? Think about what you need to be able to do with your dog. Try out a different walk, where you can let your dog off lead.

Share a picture of your dog walking on lead. Write about how you got on with the challenge below.

WEEK 15: PULLING AND LUNGING ON LEAD – PROBLEM

Problems with dog walking on lead

Last week I talked in general terms about walking dogs on lead. I talked about being realistic about managing your dog on lead. There are a number of different ways you can help manage your dog. I recommended a longline to help with your puppy's recall. You can use a harness as an alternative to a simple lead and collar. Never use a harmful device, such as a prong collar (please sign the petition).

Off lead is always best

As I said last week and often repeat, letting your dog off lead should always be your main goal when walking your dog. You should be choosing areas to walk that are generally safe. Recall is of course the most important skill to have. I realise it's a challenge! But that doesn't mean that you shouldn't work at it.

Quin is the perfect example of a dog who is better off lead. At 5 months of age, he can still be a bit worried about new situations and can 'react' when he sees a new dog, or sometimes a strange person. He barks and lunges at them. When he is off lead he can 'sort himself out'. So his reaction is much less and he calms down more quickly.

Pulling on lead

I feel that dogs pull on the lead primarily because they want to get on with the walk! Dogs tend to walk more quickly than we do. Well Border Collies do anyway. My dogs pull when they are setting out for their walk. On the way home they are much more calm. So if you are just getting to a safe place to let them off, a bit of pulling isn't really a problem.

If you do want to stop them pulling, you need to not pull back. This is pretty difficult to achieve! You need to let the lead go loose, or change direction every time they pull forward. Another tactic is to have the lead round the back of your legs so they are not in front of you (just watch the dog doesn't pull you over!) Or you can use a head collar, but dogs do hate these.

Why do dogs react?

If a dog sees something they do not know about, or understand, they react, usually by barking, growling, standing up to it, backing off or running away. Well you would, wouldn't you?

How do you feel when you are faced with a new situation? Going into a room full of strangers? Starting a new job? Being introduced to a partner's family? Scary isn't it? So you should be able to recognise that sometimes dogs can be overwhelmed, or scared. It's completely normal.

What to do if your dog reacts

When your dog reacts to a scary or new situation, there are a number of actions we can take. These include:

- nothing
- punish or shout at your dog
- reward your dog
- calm your dog
- train your dog

Don't underestimate the power of doing nothing? If you stay calm and ignore the 'scary thing', your puppy can learn that it's no big deal. Sometimes that's enough. It might even be the best course of action. Let's consider the alternatives.

Hopefully you won't punish your dog. Ironically, if you shout at your dog for barking and lunging, they might feel rewarded for their action. A shout is basically a bark, after all. So you're just joining in with the fun! If you pull on the lead, that is the same as your dog pulling on the lead! Be careful not to reward the dog's actions, because you know what will happen next, don't you? Yes, your dog will think that is what is needed.

Calm down

You might feel that you need to reassure your dog, to calm them down when something is scaring them. Sadly, this is also a reward. Your dog barks to warn you as much as anything. They lunge and look fierce to protect you. If you give them a fuss or talk to them, they can see this as a reward, or positive reinforcement, for their actions.

Train to ignore

This is ultimately the best course of action. In order to do this you need to get their attention *before* the scary thing happens or appears. You need to be able to hold their attention and reward them for paying you the attention. Training your dog in this way takes a bit of time and effort. Your reward will be a dog that can walk calmly past other dogs, runners, cyclists, cars etc. If you can't be bothered to train your puppy to do this, just ignore the barking and lunging. They might calm down anyway.

Walking on lead – conclusion

Teaching your dog to walk nicely on lead is a real challenge! Staying calm and not worrying about 'other things' is a good start. Training your dog to ignore other dogs and issues is much better. The best solution is simply to let them off lead! Ultimately, we just need our dogs to cope with varying situations, including crossing roads, changing pace and passing distractions.

Weekly Focus Challenge

What is your dog like on lead? How much have you worked on this? What issues do you have? Practise keeping their focus while other things pass you – eg cars, runners, cyclists and other dogs.

Share a picture of your dog walking on lead. Write about how you got on with the challenge below.

_____

_____

_____

_____

_____

_____

WEEK 16: KEEP REWARDING - INFORMATION

Why rewarding your dog is so important

Imagine the scene – you start a new job, it's difficult and stressful, but it's OK, you are going to get paid. You probably also get feedback from your boss and those around you. So you know you're doing a great job. Then you get paid! Fantastic, that makes it worthwhile.

Now imagine that after a few months your boss comes to see you and says "You're doing a great job, just what we want. I know you are enjoying the work, so we've decided we're not going to pay you anymore." How do you feel about your job now? Would you carry on working just as hard? Hmm.

Last week I was lucky enough to see a couple of friends with three of my (grown up) puppies. I do see lots of my pups regularly because they belong to friends, since I am not a commercial breeder/puppy farmer. Anyway, I took some photos and someone asked me how we got the dogs to 'pose' for these. I (rather flippantly) said "well they're Border Collies so of course they do as they're told!" It was a bit of an exaggeration, as six Border Collies on a new walk will obviously be pretty excited! We did have to manage them and I did have to keep my wits about me. But the main reason we are able to sit them in a line is because we *reward them!*

What is a reward?

Please remember that there are different kinds of reward, not just food. For us, we can be rewarded by money, but also by praise, or approval. We also enjoy physical praise, such as a hug or kiss from a loved one. Think about how that makes you feel? It's the same for your dog. Even a verbal 'Well done!' can be rewarding in the right context. In summary, rewards for your dog can be:

- food
- petting or stroking
- play with a toy (tugging)

- verbal praise

You might need to mix it up and offer different rewards at different times. Or use bigger rewards at different times. It is important to understand what is rewarding for your dog.

The right reward for the task

There needs to be a difference between 'an everyday reward' and a bonus. What would you get a bonus for? Usually, this will be for something extra, including an extra effort. It's the same for your dog. If you are training something, the sequence should be:

- action – reward
- action – reward
- action – reward
- bigger action – jumbo reward!

For example, if you are practising wait. You might ask for a couple of seconds' wait (reward). Then you might step away and then back in (reward). Next you might step in and out a couple of times (reward). Finally, you step away a bit further and wait a few seconds longer. If this is successful, bingo! Jumbo reward! This might be a few extra treats, or a 'release' – OK and then play.

What about when it goes wrong?

It doesn't always go right, does it? If you are practising wait and your dog moves, what should you do? Tell them off? No. Just calmly put them back into position and ask them to wait once again. Don't expect perfection (and you won't be disappointed). Reward the bits that go right and ignore the rest.

Just an aside about wait training; try not to touch your dog if they break their wait and you have to move them back to position. Touching your dog is a reward. You can't always avoid this, but the less you touch them in this case, the less confusing it is for your dog.

Be realistic

As always, be realistic about what you can achieve. Set yourself and your dog up to succeed, not to fail. Take into account their age and experience. Be pleased with what they can do. I'm telling myself this as I'm writing it by the way; it's hard to remember!

Weekly Focus Challenge

What rewards do you use with your dog? Are these things rewarding enough? Do you always remember to take treats on a walk with you? Do you find an opportunity to give your dog a reward on every walk? What about at home – do you reward your dog around the house?

Share a picture of your dog doing something for a reward. Write about how you got on with the challenge below.

_____

_____

_____

_____

_____

_____

WEEK 17: RECALL REVISITED - TRAINING

When recall stops working

Recall is the hardest thing to conquer when you have a puppy. I met someone this morning with a young Jack Russell, on lead. The owner told me her recall wasn't very good 'if she sees something else she won't come back'. What was she doing about it? Keeping her on lead. Boo. If you asked your dog, I believe they would rather be run over by a car than kept on lead their whole life. But if you put a bit of work into your recall, your dog won't be run over by a car.

Not an instant fix

Getting your dog to come back to you is *not* something you teach at the start and then have forever more. You MUST work at it, day in, day out. I have talked about it from day one, but I practise it every single time I take my dogs out. I call them. And reward them for coming. The dogs are running around and having fun, when I call Quin back to me. He comes back pretty well, going past the other dogs, who know it is not for them to come back (unless they want a sweetie!) Not a bad effort.

Recall goes wrong

I'm writing about recall again now, because at six months old, your puppy will start to change. I met someone the other day who said that their 7 month old Labrador puppy was no longer coming back to them. Ah, I said, he's 7 months old, that's why.

At around this age, puppies start to think for themselves a bit more. They become more confident and able to go a bit further away from you. They also start to realise that if they don't *immediately* come back to you, nothing bad happens. Great! So why bother? Well what's the answer? You have to be more exciting than the other thing! That can be tough to do.

Your puppy might be thinking 'what's the point?' I'll just lie down, that's something we've been practising. But your puppy will eventually realise that you mean it, so he will come. What do you do then? Smack him for being naughty and not coming back straight away? No.
Be *thrilled* that he came! You have to actually **be** thrilled (even if you are secretly wishing you could kill him). Worse will happen in the future.

When I did a video to demonstrate this point:

- My dogs are running around, off lead, next to a busy dual carriageway. They are not running into the road. Why would they? That is not the way we walk. I have shown them

over the years that we go along the path. It is a familiar route to us all. More importantly though, I pay attention to my dogs and make sure I feel under control. They can run about, I can call them.
- When Quin stops and doesn't want to come back to me, I move away from him, not towards him.

Don't chase your dog!

Who can run the fastest, you or your dog? If your dog is ten years old or more, a bit arthritic and maybe going a bit blind, AND if you are under 30 years old and regularly run marathons, you are *still* not faster than your dog! If your dog decides to run, that's it, they've gone.

So there is absolutely no point in trying to catch your dog. If your dog doesn't come towards you, you need to make yourself more interesting. That's all there is to it. Running away from your dog is a great way to achieve this.

The collar grab

Putting the lead back on at the end of a walk is a massive problem point for most people. You go for a lovely long walk and then come to put the lead back on and the dog runs away. Here are the reasons why your dog does that:

- they are not tired, the walk hasn't been long enough (they are never tired!)
- they know that it's the end of the walk because you always finish the walk there
- you expect your dog to come and sit calmly at your feet while you fiddle around with the lead
- you don't reward your dog for coming back to you.

In order to fix this, here's what you do:

1. always reward your dog for coming back to you
2. call them back to you several times *during* the walk, not just at the end. Don't forget to reward them!
3. make sure you have hold of your dog before touching the lead.
4. don't expect them to sit and wait, just grab them and put the lead on. Make sure you reward them.

NB: I don't try and hold the collar, I hold him. I grab his fur, to stroke him and make a fuss of him. That physical engagement is a reward for him, so it reinforces his desire to come back to me. I have the lead clipped around my neck, so once I have him, I can easily grab the lead and clip it on. It doesn't have to be neat, or smart. It has to work for me and reward my dog.

Trust your dog

Going back to the point above about dogs not running into the road, I honestly wish people would trust their dogs more. Of course I realise that I have Border Collies and not all breeds of dog are as fast, manic and easily scared as mine. Oh wait, were you expecting me to say as trainable, intelligent and well-behaved as mine? Hmm.

Dogs will run about. They should, it's what dogs do. But they come back. Quin still checks in with me. Even when I don't recall him. I am happy for him to be out of sight, knowing that he will come back to me.

Let recall go wrong

Nobody's perfect. Not even me. Lol. So it won't go right all the time. It shouldn't though, we don't learn unless we experience problems. Please, please let your dog go through it. If you don't give them a chance, how can they get better?

Don't forget, there are plenty of safe ways you can practice and reward your recall. Call your dog around the house. Call them in from the garden. When you are out, start with letting them go to the end of a longline, or extendable lead and recalling them.

If you really are a scaredy-cat, just go somewhere you feel secure and practice. Don't just go to a field and let your dog run about. RECALL THEM! and reward. Reward. Reward. Honestly, your dog will thank you for it.

Weekly Focus Challenge

Where are you up to with your recall? Make a note of how your dog responds when you call him. What do you do when he comes back? How often do you call him? Why does it go wrong? What do you do about it? If you don't let him off lead, please find a way to practise this NOW. The longer you leave it, the harder it will be to let go.

Share a picture of your dog running around off lead. Write about how you got on with the challenge below.

WEEK 18: LEAVE IT! - PROBLEM

Responding to temptation – teaching your dog to leave something alone

How do you teach your dog not to pick up *everything*? That's the challenge I'm faced with at the moment. It sometimes feels as though every time I set eyes on Quin he is eating something. I've just been reading about 6 month-old puppies who have trashed their houses and gardens. That's a bit of a shame and not very good for the dog.

Dogs need boundaries

There is nothing wrong with teaching a dog (or a child) that they cannot do exactly as they please. Not everything in the world is good, or safe, or for them. 'No' should be in your dog's vocabulary, even if they (hopefully) don't hear it very often. Yes we should be training with positivity and rewards, but we still need to teach them 'stop', 'wait' and 'no', or 'leave it!' Imagine you are taking your medication and you drop a tablet on the floor. You don't want your dog eating it do you?

Common foods toxic to dogs

You can see from this list that there are some really common foods that are really poisonous for dogs. Grapes and raisins are seriously dangerous and require a vet visit. But I'm sure you, like me eat raisins regularly. Of course other foods are less of a problem – who eats chocolate after all :p.

How to teach 'leave it' to your dog

It's not hard. Just say 'leave it!' like you mean it. Quite loudly, quite sharply. Your dog should pause and look at you in surprise. You then need to quickly call them away, or grab them, or grab whatever it is your dog shouldn't have.

As with every other bit of training your dog, you will have much more success if you reward your dog! If you make it a really fantastic thing to leave the tasty treat on the floor and come back to you, they are definitely more likely to remember the lesson and the associated command.

Temptation Alley

You can also try a 'temptation alley' exercise. This is also great for focusing your recall! These are sometimes set up at fun dog shows, for you to test out your dog. It's hilarious to see some dogs thinking 'Bonanza!' and gobbling everything in sight on their way to you. NB: if you have a Labrador, they will *always* eat all the treats before getting to you. This exercise is also used at puppy training classes, to test recall and help you be more exciting. It's part of the KC Good Citizen Award. For example, at the silver level:

Food Manners

The object of this exercise is for the dog to have good manners when aware of food. Food should be handled or consumed while the dog, on a loose lead, is taken in close proximity to it. The dog should not unduly respond to this temptation, i.e. not to beg for food or steal.

Teaching your dog *not* to do something is much harder than teaching them to do something. Don't despair! You can do this. Your dog will thank you (and so will your vet).

Weekly Focus Challenge

Can you persuade your dog to leave something when they go to eat it? If not, now is the time to work on this with them. Think about how you manage your dog around food. Do they beg? Do you put them away when you are eating? What about when you feed them – is this easy to manage? Or could it be better?

Share a picture of your dog ignoring a treat on the floor and looking at you. Write about how you got on with the challenge below.

WEEK 19: VET VISITS – INFORMATION

How to prepare your dog for a visit to the vet

Nobody likes taking their dog to the vet. It is definitely one of the worst things about owning a dog – coping with them being ill. We love our dogs and we want the absolute best for them, so deciding when to go to see a vet can be the first obstacle.

Is it serious?

Here are a few reasons why you need to visit your vet's:

- Vaccinations/boosters – I've talked elsewhere about the importance of vaccinating your dog. Just as with people, it is life-saving and simple.
- Annual check-up – this is usually part of having their booster done and is equally important as it gives you a chance to discuss any minor issues with your vet
- Sickness and diarrhoea – probably the most common reason for visiting a vet. When you have owned dogs for many years you will know that dogs are sick pretty often and it is not an immediate cause for concern. It's usually because they have eaten something they shouldn't have done. Throwing up once solves it – no further action required. When it persists and/or is accompanied by diarrhoea, there is a need to take action. Again, experience shows that starving for 24 hours might solve it, or feeding a plain food like boiled rice.

Princesses are rarely sick

A vet is essential if there is accompanying lethary, if the coat is 'staring' ie not shiny, but dull and flat. You should also go to the surgery if you know that something toxic has been eaten (raisins or chocolate for example). Or if you know that an object has been eaten (usually if you have a Labrador this will be the reason and socks will be involved).

You should be aware of the clinical signs of pancreatitis, as this is relatively common and requires hospital treatment. The most common clinical signs include **nausea, vomiting, fever, lethargy, abdominal pain, diarrhoea, and decreased appetite**.

- Injury – either self-inflicted or caused by others. This mainly includes any sign of limping or change in mobility. Again, experience may mean you can check for a cause (a thorn perhaps?) Or wait and see if it's just a bruise or underlying muscle damage. You will gradually learn how tolerant your dog is of pain and whether they are behaving differently as a result of this injury. Sometimes rest is what is needed.

- Older dogs require more frequent care and management. Cat the Vet talks about managing our older dogs and asks people to fill in a survey about it. You would be amazed at how much care older dogs can take! Arthritis is probably the most common issue, but most dogs over the age of ten are on at least one type of medication.

Anxiety around vet visits is very common

Why do dogs get anxious when going to the vet? After all, they start off by going just for a check-up and a vaccination. I believe this is mainly because we are nervous. So when you go into your vet's practice, please try and relax? Try taking a breath before getting your dog out of the car? Better still, go and book in without your dog, then fetch them and go back in. Talk to the receptionists, who are always lovely. Take a moment to look around and see the setup, admire the toys for sale and see how the waiting area is arranged.

Dogs who don't often interact with other dogs may feel really stressed by being in close proximity to other dogs, particularly if they are feeling unwell. If the waiting area is busy, wait outside with your dog and ask to be called in when they are ready to see you. Of course this has been happening anyway throughout the pandemic, but I have to assume when writing this that things are returning to more standard practice.

Treats on hand
As with everything else you do with your dog, make sure you reward them for being there. My dogs know that they get treats just for sitting in the waiting area. This morning Luna knew that if she stood on the scales she would get a reward, so she got weighed three times! Bless her.

You can't reward every few minutes with treats, so make sure you make a fuss of your dog and talk to them. All of this should help you to feel calm as well.

The examination
When you get called into the consultation room, you need to be positive about going in, so your dog stays happy too. You need to chat to the vet about what is wrong and then be prepared for your dog to be examined.

I'm sure you spend ages every day fussing and stroking your dog, but how often do you examine them? You need them to be comfortable with you doing this, so that a vet can also do it. The more often you handle your dog in this way, the more relaxed they (and you) will be in the vet's. Don't forget the reward!

Visits without treatment

If you are passing your vet's surgery, you might like to pop in to say hello and have your dog weighed. Again, the pandemic notwithstanding, you may not be able to do this if it is busy. But it's worth taking your dog in, standing them on the scales, giving them a reward and leaving. Nice and calm, a positive experience for you both.

The final vet visit

Over 90% of dogs are euthanised. It's the inevitable conclusion to living with our best friend. We know that when they are suffering, it is far better to let them go, in peace, than to prolong their agony. Fortunately, our very brave and highly qualified vets are able to make this process simple and painless for our beloved dogs.

Please do make the effort to stay with your dog at this time? It is far better for your dog and actually much better for you. Death is part of life, so you should let them go off to sleep in the arms of their most loved person. I'll stop there. RIP my beautiful Sunshine, Quin's grandmother, gone in March 2021. With thanks to my vets at Milton Keynes Veterinary Group, who take such good care of us all.

Weekly Focus Challenge

How have the vet visits with your dog gone so far? Have you gone in with your dog, just to get them used to going? Stand them on the scales, give them a treat, buy them a toy (if you can afford it!) and then leave. Or better still, get some of the staff to give your dog a fuss and a treat. The vet's is a lovely place where good things happen!

Share a picture of your being good. Write about how you got on with the challenge below.

WEEK 20: FETCH THE BALL! – TRAINING

Teaching your dog to play fetch

Why do we play fetch with our dog? Usually so that they get to run around and tire themselves out, whilst we can sit in the garden and look at our phones, or wander along slowly in the park and look at our phones. Before we consider how to teach our dog to play fetch, or retrieve, let's think about our motivation and the actual benefits to the dog?

The benefits of playing fetch

Dogs do absolutely *love* playing fetch, on the whole. Once they get going, some dogs are difficult to stop! Throwtheball, throwtheball, throwtheball! That's certainly the catchphrase of many Border Collies. My dogs generally play with toys for some periods every day and will demand these are thrown for them, as well as playing tug and chewing on other toys, some of which may be designed for chewing.

It can be very stimulating and entertaining for some dogs. It can get them up and moving, running about and chasing. Sometimes this can be more entertaining than just going for a walk. Lots of people throw balls or toy sticks whilst out walking, as this makes sure that a dog on its own has a bit of a runabout.

Help with recall

Throwing a ball is definitely a way to keep your dog focused on you. If your dog's recall is not that great, try taking a favourite, squeaky toy with you. When the dog starts wandering off, try squeaking the toy and waving it around excitedly. Then when your dog looks round, say 'Get it!' and throw it a short distance away. Your dog should go and get the toy and may then come back to you to have it thrown again. Remember to be exciting!

The downsides of fetch

When I was a child, we threw sticks for our dogs. It's an obvious thing to do, as dogs love chewing sticks and will often pick these up instinctively. However, we now know that sticks are a really BAD IDEA. They can easily splinter and get stuck in a dog's throat, choking them or causing horrific injuries.

A simple shift has been made, to ensure that we don't cause these injuries to our dogs. We know that this is what happens when we throw sticks, so we don't throw these any more. Instead, we throw tennis balls. We often use a ball chucker, or thrower. Again, these seemed like a great way to get that extra bit of running around.
Sadly, these have also been shown to be more than a dog needs. Too much intense running, jumping and turning can, you've guessed it, cause injuries to our dogs. So if you want to throw a ball, that's fine, but not to excess. Likewise, frisbees are not brilliant, as the dog is leaping around after them.

Managing fetch play with your dog

You can strike a happy medium. This morning Aura found a tennis ball on our walk. Happy day! I popped it into my pocket until we were in the open part of the park. Then I lobbed it a short distance away. Aura brings it back to me and I try and kick it away, without her 'saving' it. A great game. She loves running around with the ball in her mouth.

Busy loves to steal the ball if it comes past her. She will then circle Aura until she thinks Aura is not paying attention, when Busy drops it and hopes it won't be found. Hilarious!

How to teach a retrieve or fetch

1. Start at home, in the house or garden. Have some treats as well as the toy and a quiet space, so your dog can concentrate.
2. You might start by getting them interested in the toy. Wave it around, holding it out of reach. Squeak it, if it has a squeaker.
3. Next, try playing a bit of a tug game with the toy. You want your dog to *really want it.*
4. Then try throwing it a few feet away. Stand still, waiting to see what your dog does. If they go over to the toy, say 'Yes!' and give them a treat.
5. Keep rewarding your dog for looking at the toy, going near it, sniffing it, and touching it. After giving a 'Yes!' and a treat, pick the toy up and wave it around, making it interesting again.
6. Once you have generated interest in the toy and your dog is going towards it, you need to wait for them to pick it up.

7. When they pick it up, call them – 'Quin come!' Usually they will then drop the toy and come back to you for a reward. That's fine. Reward the dog, then throw the toy again.
8. Keep going, and they will gradually get more excited and start bringing the toy nearer to you.
9. Finally, the dog will bring the toy to you and either give it to you, or drop it at your feet. The next bit is up to you.

Aura will only bring the toy to my feet and is not brilliant at doing that. The others will give toys to me to throw. If you want it put into your hand, your dog needs to be really motivated for you to throw it and you need to be patient. One of the funniest experiences I've had was teaching Sunny to put the toy in my hand. She used to throw the ball near me and then look up expectantly, waiting for the next throw.

I was at a training class and the trainer said, "Put your hand out and wait." I waited. And waited. Sunny kept looking at me and barking, then picking up the ball and throwing it near me. I kept my hand out, moving it a bit to get her attention. Sunny completely lost her temper and starting shouting at me "You pick it up, it's just there! Why are you so lazy! Just throw it for me!" Honestly, it was hilarious. Eventually she put it in my hand. But she always got cross if I demanded she do that.

When to end the game

NB: If the dog doesn't want to give the toy back, try offering a treat in exchange for the toy. Or another toy in exchange. If that doesn't work, turn away, game over. When the dog does eventually drop the toy, you can pick it up and be exciting again. The object of the game is to play with your dog – it needs to be fun for them too.

When your dog is reluctant to give the toy back, it is often because they have had enough. Some dogs can only handle two or three turns at fetch. Take note of their level of fitness and how stimulated they are. Try not to overdo it?

Formal retrieve and fetch for assistance dogs

If you go to formal obedience training with your dog, or if you have a gundog and want to train them to retrieve, there are different elements you will need to work on. In formal obedience, a dog will need to wait, then go and fetch a dumbbell, picking it up cleanly, bringing it straight back to you, presenting it by seating neatly in front of you and then finishing in the heel position.

Gundogs have to be able to retrieve game from long distance and by going over or through obstacles. Assistance dogs have to be able to pick up and retrieve a wide range of obstacles, such as keys, TV remote controls, phones and clothing. Lots of fun to be had!

Weekly Focus Challenge

Can you play fetch with your dog? Or play a game with a toy? Try teaching them to bring a toy back to you. Some dogs are really not interested – that's fine.

Share a picture of your dog fetching a toy. Write about how you got on with the challenge below.

_____
_____
_____
_____
_____
_____

WEEK 21: GUARDING FOOD/TOYS – PROBLEM

How to cope when your dog guards food or toys

You know I'm old, so I grew up being told that under no circumstances should you interfere with your dog when they are eating. You knew that if you tried to stroke it or even go near it, you might lose your hand! Nice. I have to say that if you leant over me and tried to take food off my plate you might lose your hand too. So is that OK? Well, yes and no.

I think it is important to respect your dog and their space. Dogs must absolutely be able to get away from a situation that makes them uncomfortable. That might be to a quiet corner, or a bed, or a crate. Border Collies definitely love a dark corner.

When guarding becomes a problem

My dogs definitely do have favourite toys or bones. They might lie down with one tucked between their front feet, or under their head. Of course if someone has something they think is great, another dog will inevitably come along and try to take it off them. Usually that's fine. Aura will absolutely complain if Quin wants to take something she has, but she won't do anything, it's just noise. I will tell him off – 'Quin! Leave Aura alone!' but I won't do anything, it's fine. If Aura went for him though, I might intervene. I would call Quin away from her and shout at them both 'Enough!' If there was a real argument over toys and it happened on more than one occasion, I would make sure I didn't leave them alone together.

Of course the biggest problem is when your dog won't give something up to you. If they take something they shouldn't, whether that is clothes or food, and then growl or snap if you try to take it, that is definitely something you need to work through.

Be careful!

Dogs are powerful predators and can be vicious if provoked. So mind how you go if your dog is challenging you for something. Don't rush in and try and grab the object off them; you will probably lose! First of all, play with your dog? Not when they are guarding something, but *before that happens.* If you regularly have engagement and interaction with your dog, they are much more likely to trust you and feel happier about you handling them.

When your dog plays with toys, you should be able to get the toy off them to throw it, or play some more. If you find this difficult, you need to try swapping the toy for a treat. Once this pattern is established, you are more likely to be able to do this with other articles.

No punishments, please

When your dog is doing something it is not supposed to, the temptation is to:
- shout
- grab
- chase
- smack

Unfortunately, this doesn't work for the dog. They are not able to understand the complex relationship between their actions and the consequences you have decided are appropriate. They won't remember what happened last time and decide not to do something in case that happens again. Or if the punishment is severe, they might remember and make sure it doesn't happen again by preparing to bite if approached. When should you punish your dog? Never. It's your fault if they have something they shouldn't.

Reward, reward, reward

My advice? Start by calling your dog away from the unwanted behaviour, to come to you and receive a treat or other reward. You might need to do this extra positively! Wow, how amazing, you came to me! Reward! If that doesn't work (it probably won't) you need something more tempting. Yummy sausage? Squeaky toy? You running away shrieking excitedly? Try everything.

Food manners

Personally, I give my dogs their food and they eat it. That's it. I put it down in the same order, in the same place, at the same time. No tricks required. No funny business. I have to give Luna her insulin, so I don't have time to mess around. If you want to be able to pick up their bowl, in case you gave them the wrong food, for example, start by adding extra food to the bowl. Or throw some food near the bowl, wait for the dog to go for that, then pick up the bowl.

Be patient. Manage your own behaviour and expectations. I think you need to be calm, quiet and confident if you want to go near your dog's food. If you are worried about doing it, don't bother?

NB: DO NOT ALLOW CHILDREN TO INTERFERE WITH YOUR DOG WHILST IT IS EATING!

Yes, many dogs will tolerate their family members taking their food and toys, just as Aura lets Quin do it to her, but honestly, don't push your luck?

Practice makes perfect

In conclusion, here are my tips for preventing food and toy guarding:
- Play with your dog regularly
- Handle them daily
- Practice 'leave it'
- Swap the item for a treat
- Throw food nearby and wait
- Call the dog away
- Stay calm and quiet

Weekly Focus Challenge

How is your dog around toys and food – have you seen any guarding behaviour? What about when you feed them – is this easy to manage? Or could it be better? Try giving them a treat in exchange for something, or calling them away and then picking it up. The more of a challenge this is, the more you need to work through it.

Share a picture of your dog relaxed and happy around a favourite toy. Write about how you got on with the challenge below.

_____

_____

_____

_____

_____

WEEK 22: GROOMING YOUR DOG – INFORMATION

Grooming: how do you keep your dog in tip top condition?

I'm revisiting this information, which I wrote a few years ago. I suspect the prices for grooming your dog have gone up considerably! Grooming is one of the key 'hidden costs' of dog ownership, as you may not think about it before you get a dog. However, once you've had your dog for a few months, you will start to realise just how much care you dog needs.

Ask yourself: how lazy am I? Then ask yourself: how rich am I? I think these are the two key questions when considering what dog will suit you. This is particularly important when thinking about the care your dog will need relating to its grooming requirements.

Long or short coat?

It doesn't take a rocket scientist to understand that dogs with short coats require less care than dogs with long coats. Common sense tells us that a Labrador will not need as much grooming as a Border Collie, for example. Or will it? Labradors have what is known as a 'shedding coat' which comes out all the time, scattering fine, short hairs throughout the house, sticking to every surface and getting into food.

As a result, short-haired dogs still need grooming. Regular brushing will stop the hair being scattered everywhere. You will also find that short-haired dogs tend to smell more, because dirt becomes trapped in the hair, prompting the need for more regular baths. Dogs like the Spanish Water Dog, Spaniels and Labradors also love the water, so will find puddles and ponds to jump into at every available opportunity.

Moulting coats

Border Collies have a 'moulting coat', which comes out in armfuls once or twice a year. Over a three week period, you will have 'tumbleweeds' around the house and may have to vacuum behind the sofas. After that, not much hair comes out. If you brush during those three weeks you can definitely reduce the impact, although you will be astonished with just how much hair comes from one dog!

Other care required for a Border Collie, (as with most dogs) will include:

- Nail trimming – their nails must be clipped or trimmed
- cutting out tats – sometimes Border Collies get hair clumped into tats, which have to be cut out. This is partly because they don't need brushing on a daily basis. Their hair is silky and usually sorts itself out, but sometimes the fine hair on the belly and round the back legs needs tidying up.

Hypoallergenic or 'non-moulting' coat

This sounds ideal doesn't it? A soft, cuddly coat, that doesn't shed or moult – perfect! Or is it? Well, in my view, there are a number of issues with this type of coat:

- it will still come out, just not as much as with shedding or moulting breeds
- you aren't guaranteed this type of coat if you have a crossbreed, or so-called designer dog – it will depend on how the mix of breeds comes out in your individual dog
- dogs with these coats need regular care. As with collies, their hair will form tats and because it is curly, this is going to happen all over their bodies, on a regular basis. They will therefore need daily brushing, and/or frequent trips to the grooming parlour.

NB: Dogs LIKE to be muddy! You won't keep them clean and that's as it should be. They need to be outside, running around, smelling smells and exploring. If you try and cover up their 'dog smell' with your silly perfumes and shampoos, they will just go and roll in some more mud.

Using a Grooming Service

I picked up a leaflet for one of these services recently, having never really looked into it before. Wow, these things cost A LOT of money! Prices are from 2018. For example:

- Pug: Bath, brush and blow dry every 4-6 weeks and Express groom every 6-8 weeks. Total annual cost: **£528**

- Cockapoo: Bath, brush and blow dry every 4-6 weeks and Full groom every 6-8 weeks. Total annual cost: **£594**
- Newfoundland: Full groom every 6-8 weeks, including de-shedding or hand stripping as required. Total annual cost: **£816**

By way of contrast:

- Border Collie: Stand in a bucket when muddy, clip nails if not worn out by running around, cut out some tats, brush when moulting. Total annual cost **£0**. Lol.

Grooming tools

Of course there are many grooming tools to choose from to enable you to do the expensive stuff yourself.   This deshedding tool looks great and it comes in different colours!

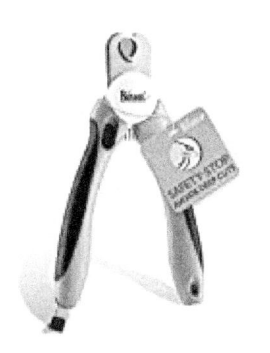

There are also nail clippers to keep their toes trim. People worry about doing their dog's nails because if you catch the quick, they bleed profusely. But the dogs aren't especially bothered if this happens, and it's much better to risk that than to have nails that are far too long, as this can be crippling for your dog.

Microchipping

Just a minor point here about microchipping, as the 'grooming service' I looked at offers to do this. **Since 6th April 2016, all dogs are required by law to be microchipped. As a breeder, I know that I am legally required to have my puppies microchipped by the time they are 8 weeks old.** I get this done by the vet. I have to register the pups in my name and then the new owners have to transfer ownership to them.

So, if you are getting a puppy, check before you get it that they have been chipped? You should therefore be able to trace its ownership back to the breeder. If you are getting a rescue dog, they should now be microchipped before you get them and that chip should be registered to the previous owner. If not, why not? There's not much point having a legal requirement to microchip dogs if this doesn't allow us to trace ownership of them.

Weekly Focus Challenge

Do you need to groom your dog? How easy is this to do? If you struggle to do anything for your dog, trying getting them into a good position with rewards, but without actually trying to do anything to them.

Share a picture of your dog before and after grooming. Write about how you got on with the challenge below.

WEEK 23: DOWN! – TRAINING

Why do we need a 'down' command?

Down is one of the first commands I teach my puppies and I have already demonstrated and talked about teaching it. As with lots of activities you do with your dog, it is not a quick fix. It takes plenty of time and practice, which is why I am revisiting it now.

First of all, lying down is much easier for your dog to do than sitting. A sit is not a particularly natural physical position for a dog – they are much more likely to lie down to wait for you. If you want a good solid 'wait', then a down is a good starting point. A dog will wait much longer and be more relaxed if you ask them to wait in a down position.

Teaching your dog a 'down' command

In order to teach a down command, start in the house, when everything else is quiet and calm. Get your dog's attention and give them a treat. What for? Well for being your wonderful dog of course! When they are focused on you, hold a treat in your hand and bring it from their nose to the floor, slowly. They should follow you down and with a bit of luck and patience, go into a down position. Yes! Reward!

Do it again. And again. And again. When you feel they are starting to understand, add the word you want to use – 'Down!' Try to use one simple word, in the same intonation, with the same emphasis. Be consistent.

Once they understand that this is the game we are playing, you can start to wait for them to go into the down, without you moving your hand in front of their nose. If they don't do it on command, carry on with the physical prompt. Some dogs always need this.

Use the right word

Lots of people say 'Lay down' when they want their dog to go into a down position. This annoys me intensely, because it is grammatically incorrect. 'Lie down' is the correct term. But I wouldn't say that anyway, because it is two words. One clear word is much easier to understand.

Not to be confused with 'Off!' as a command. Again, lots of people say 'down' to their dog when it jumps up. I say 'Off' to distinguish between these two actions. I do also say 'off' when the dogs are on the sofa and I want to sit down, but they mainly understand this because I am waving my hand at them and sitting on top of them if they don't move. Lol.

If you get confused trying to stick to different words for different commands, don't do agility! We need an increasing number of words in this dog sport. 'Tunnel' is no longer sufficient – we need 'wrong end of tunnel' as well. Hmm.

Increase the distance

The ultimate goal with the down is to have the dog 'drop' when they are at a distance from you. I will talk about this more a bit later on, but it is really useful way to control your dog. If they will drop into a down where they are, you can stop them from running into a road, charging into another dog, blocking the path for a cyclist and so on. You will earn the admiration of everyone, who will describe your dog as 'well trained' and 'beautifully behaved'. It's just a down command. How do you teach this?

How do you think? Yes, of course, practice it a thousand times. Top tip: it really helps a puppy to learn down at a distance if they have other dogs to copy. Once one drops, they all do. Eventually.

Weekly Focus Challenge

How quickly can you get your dog to lie down? Do you always need food to tempt them down? Do you need to bring your hand down in front of your dog? Or can they do it just on a verbal command alone? Practise this a few (hundred) times and see if you can get it quicker and more consistent.

Share a picture of your dog in a down position. Write about how you got on with the challenge below.

WEEK 24: DISOBEDIENCE - PROBLEM

What does your dog understand?

Your dog understands when you ask them to do something, if you are clear and consistent. For example, if you say 'sit' they should sit. Or they should go into a down on command, as discussed last week. But imagine saying to your dog "Now I'm just off upstairs and I'm leaving this food item on the side, so don't eat it, OK?" What will they get from that? Hmm. Likewise, if you say to your dog "Why did you eat that food I left on the side? You know it wasn't your food!" Can you honestly think that your dog will grasp your meaning?

Dogs will listen to you going 'blah blah blah' and not take much notice. Unless you say their name. Or 'biscuit'. Or 'sausage'. They are good at picking out key words. Research has shown that dogs understand around 200 words. Pretty clever. But we say around 5000 words PER DAY! Well, women do anyway.

Body language

Dogs are *really* good at understanding is body language. If you have a deaf dog, as many people with elderly dogs do have (or if you have a dog with white hair, such as a Dalmatian) you can teach it sign language relatively easily. This is mainly because dogs really focus on how we are moving and pick up on subtle cues and expressions.

Amazingly, dogs are able to read our facial expressions, even though their own expressions can look very different. They know what our angry face looks like and how we become tense, making ourselves tall and threatening. They react to that, cowering away in fear.

Try taking the time to understand what your dog is saying to you. Looking at the chart, can you see where it says 'your dog is lying to you'? Or the picture of the dog planning something naughty? Have you heard about the dog that that is unkind? No.

Dogs are not mean!

The reason we love dogs so much is because they are pretty straightforward creatures. Your dog will not *try* and annoy you. Their goal in life is to please you, so that you will feed them, fuss them and keep them company. If a dog is aggressive, it is nearly always afraid.

Quick quiz for you

After all that, when do you think you should punish your dog? Here's a quick quiz for you:

Question 1
Your year old puppy drinks lots of river water while on a walk, then pees in the house. Do you:

a) Rub her nose it, whilst shouting at her
b) Go and smack her
c) Sigh and clear it up
d) Remind yourself not to let her drink too much when it's hot?

Question 2
Your dog runs off out of sight whilst on a walk. Do you:

a) Call him positively and excitedly, squeaking a toy.
b) Wait for him to come back
c) Chase after him, angrily shouting his name
d) Remind yourself that you need to carry on working on his recall training, although he is much better than he was?

Question 3
Your young dog jumps up at your husband when he gets home from work and jumps up at visitors. Do you:

a) Give her a smack and shout at her for being naughty
b) Push her off and say 'Down!' at her
c) Ask your husband and visitors to turn away from her and ignore her
d) Remind yourself that you need to ask people to help you continue her jumping up training and explain what you want?

Question 4
You leave your sandwich on a coffee table while you go to the toilet. You are only gone for a minute, but your dog eats your food. Do you:

a) Wonder where your sandwich could be

b) Yell at your dog for eating your food
   c) Smack your dog to teach it a lesson
   d) Remind yourself that if you leave food in front of a dog, it will only *not* eat it if it is ill?

Question 5
Your children love playing with your dog but struggle to leave him alone. One of your children comes over and puts her face up to the dog's (whilst he is on his bed) and your dog growls. Do you:

   a) Praise the dog for being patient with your child
   b) Shout at your child for getting in the dog's face
   c) Smack your dog for growling at your child
   d) Remind yourself to work with your child and your dog about good interaction and to make sure that you never leave them alone together?

Question 6
Your dog snaps at another dog that comes into her face when you are out on a walk. The owner of the other dog calls out "it's OK he's friendly" but your dog growls and shows her teeth. Do you:

   a) Shout at the owner of the other dog
   b) Give your dog a treat for not killing the other dog
   c) Smack your dog and shout at her for being aggressive
   d) Remind yourself to work on distracting distracting your dog away from approaching dogs and reward them for ignoring other dogs?

Question 7
You leave your dog out in the garden for a while. When you come back there is a big hole in the middle of the lawn. Do you:

   a) Beat the dog for being so naughty
   b) Punish the dog by shutting them away for a few hours
   c) Drag the dog to the hole and yell at them
   d) Remind yourself not to leave the dog unsupervised and bored where they can do damage?

Question 8
You come in to find your dog has chewed one of your trainers. Do you:

   a) Ring the rescue centre because you are sick of the bloody dog
   b) Shout at the dog
   c) Show the dog the shoe and give him a smack

d) Remind yourself to buy some more dog toys and to tidy your shoes away in future?

I am hoping that you have enjoyed my bit of fun? Of course we can all get fed up with our annoying dogs and all their bad behaviours. However, I hope you can see that it is important to manage our expectations and to understand that any dog is still a dog. How well your puppy behaves is entirely up to you and the way you manage them. Some dogs are easier to train than others, but none of them need punishment.

Weekly Focus Challenge

When has your dog been disobedient? What did you do? What should you have done? What will you do next time?

Share a picture of your dog being good. Write about how you got on with the challenge below.

WEEK 25: THE TEENAGE PHASE - INFORMATION

Coping with your puppy's hormones and the teenage phase

Do as I say, not as I do! Last week I talked about why you should *not* tell your puppy off. Today I could have cheerfully killed mine! Aargh! Such a naughty little shit. My family were trying to make me laugh about it by telling me about this great blog post explaining why you shouldn't tell off your puppy. I told them that shouting at him made me feel better.

What did he do? He climbed over the back of the sofa onto the sideboard, dug some soil out of a plant pot, (having already killed off the plant that was in there last week). And he got one of my Christmas gnomes and de-stuffed it. Thanks Quin.

Why does your puppy's behaviour get worse?

When they begin to reach sexual maturity, your puppy goes through what is known as the 'teenage phase'. I remember a couple of years ago, one of my puppy owners saying to me "When do they stop being difficult and annoying?" I (unhelpfully) replied "Around two years of age." Hopefully it's not quite that bad.

At two years of age, you have a fully-formed adult dog. From six months old though, you have an adult-sized dog with a puppy's mind. They are still bouncy, lively, playful, untrained and annoying. They still chew, destroy things, demand attention and generally fill up more time than you have. And their hormones are raging!

This is the age that things can go a bit backwards, to be honest. That fantastic recall? Not so much now. Am I bothered? I have better things to do. You know how we worked so hard to ignore other dogs? Well now I'm going to bark at them. Or chase them off. Or play with them. And when you call me, I won't hear you. Little bugger.

New anxieties

Quin misbehaved this morning and last weekend because he was left unsupervised. There were other dogs in the room, but I went upstairs (to do some cycling) and I thought he would be OK. Nope. So although he doesn't have the mindset to think 'What can I do to really piss her off?' he *does* feel a bit anxious and lonely and look around for something to do. I suppose it's possible that me telling him off will make him decide not to do it again.

Much more likely that he won't do it again because I have:

- moved the (now plantless) plant pot outside
- moved the sofa further from the sideboard
- asked other family to stay with him while I go upstairs
- taken him with me when I'm working or exercising
- put him in his crate if I do go out
- make sure he practises being on his own.

Dogs suffer from 'separation anxiety'; they get stressed if left alone. This is particularly true if they normally have company. They may have been fine for months, but as they get older they learn to depend on you more for company and care more when you are not around.
Dealing with separation anxiety is possible, but as with everything else, it takes work.

Keep practising to cope with hormones

As I prepare to watch the final of Strictly Come Dancing I think about the amount of work it takes those celebrities to achieve what they do. That catchphrase 'Keeeeep Dancing!' is at the heart of the high standards of performance. And my friend Sam has just won a jumping agility class at the Horse of the Year show (they have dogs too). I know the level of dedication she has for training and working with her dogs.

Basically, the more effort you make, the better behaved your dog will be. I've been pretty distracted recently, with all the usual Christmas crap we have to do. As a result, my puppy is not as well-behaved as he should be! So, keeeep training!

Don't give up on your puppy

Puppies are most commonly re-homed around 6-8 months of age. The Blue Cross say *"the most common reason for dogs needing our help to find them a new home is that their previous owner no longer had the time to care for a pet."* However, what this means is that people just cannot be bothered to keep on training the bloody annoying puppy. So they give up. Which is a shame, because in just a few more months you will have that dog you dreamed of having. Won't we Quin?

Weekly Focus Challenge

What does your dog do that drives you mad? Is that a phase or an ongoing problem that needs to be fixed?

Share a picture of your dog being good. Write about how you got on with the challenge below.

WEEK 26: CELEBRATING 6 MONTHS!

Let's celebrate! How well do you know your puppy?

Can you believe it? I've had Quin for 6 months! He's my 9th dog and my third boy, so I haven't had many surprises, but if you've just spent 6 months with your first dog, how's it been? Let's celebrate the successes and reflect on what still needs a bit more work?

If you've spent time with your dog, you should know them pretty well, right? Ah but how much time to you *consciously* spend time with them. This morning I was doing some focused work on Quin's recall, which has deteriorated bang on time, as his hormones kick in and he enters the teenage stage.

So here we go, how much do you know about your dog?

Around the house
1. What is your dog's favourite food? Are they a good eater? Do they need to be slowed down when eating? Quin is a steady eater and always finishes his food. I'm happy with his weight and the firmness of his poo.
2. What treats or snacks does your dog like? Raw carrot is a favourite of my dogs. They all love crisps and will offer lots of tricks to win these!
3. Where does your dog like to sleep? Do they go on the sofa or your bed? Or do they prefer to find a quiet corner? I'm putting money on the fact they don't often sleep in that expensive bed you bought? My dogs like a raised bed with some lovely vet bed on it. They usually just lie on the floor.
4. When does your dog wake up in the morning? What time do they go to bed? Does this work well with your routine? It's hard work changing your dog's body clock isn't it?
5. How often does your dog need to go out to toilet? Do they always go in the same place? Do they prefer to toilet in the garden or on a walk? I like my dogs to be able to toilet in the garden, so that I don't have to take them out – it's so much more convenient. But I know they prefer to toilet on a walk. So I make sure I pick up after them in the garden as well as on walks and I walk them after breakfast so they can toilet then.

Out and about

6. How often do you take your dog out for a walk? Do you go at the same time each day? For the same length of time? My dogs have an hour long walk, off lead, around an hour after their breakfast, from 7.30 am.
7. Where does your dog like walking? Do you go to different places, or do the same trudge every day? Dogs love variety and thrive on visiting different walks. My dogs love the woods! So many interesting smells.
8. Where else have you taken your dog? Have they been to the pub? Or to a cafe? It's a good to show off your dog and give them a different experience. Quin went to the pub a few times back in the summer and was a good boy.
9. Have you visited someone else's home with your dog? Don't be afraid to take them into new situations? Quin recently went into school and behaved himself brilliantly!
10. I know this is a tricky question in the current climate, but have you taken your dog away? Quin has been up to Scotland and down to Devon – he loves it!

Tricks and games

11. Can your dog do the basics? Sit, down, wait? How often do you practise these? Every few days is a good starting point.
12. How is your dog's recall? How often do you practise this? As I said at the top, Quin's recall is currently going through a dodgy phase and definitely needs extra work.
13. Can your dog do any other tricks? Quin does this really cute 'roll over and die' trick when I point at him and say 'Bang!' He can also do a 'twist' which is pretty easy to teach.
14. What's your dog's favourite game to play with you? If you have other dogs, do they play together and what games do they play? Quin loves to play tuggy and will bring me a toy to get me engaged. He also loves to play tug with Ounce, but he plays rough and tumble with Busy.
15. Does your dog engage with other dogs when out on walks? Do they try and say hello nicely, or bounce into other dogs' faces? Quin is wary with other dogs, but annoyingly barks at dogs on lead. He does occasionally engage with another dog with a bit of chase. He's cautious, but not aggressive, so that's not too bad at this age.

Training and activities

16. What classes have you done with your puppy? Did you do a 6-8 week block of puppy classes? What did you learn? Quin didn't go to puppy classes because he is my 8th dog – I could run the classes! I did consciously try to cover the areas.

17. Did you continue with classes after the initial block? Was the trainer good? Did you find it useful spending time with other people with pups the same age as yours? I think that's one of the best things about going to training – knowing you are not alone!
18. Have you tried out other types of training? Quin has been to a few scentwork classes. He found it quite hard being in a classroom for an hour, but was perfectly capable of doing the training.
19. Hoopers is a great way to introduce your dog to the skills you need for agility. If you plan to do agility, you need to get onto a waiting list, as trainers are hard to find and often fully booked. You can't start agility properly until they are a year old, but there is plenty of foundation work you can do.
20. Obedience training is another way to challenge you and your dog and build on your working relationship.

Health and breeding

21. How typical is your dog for its breed? Or breeds? If they are a crossbreed, can you see traits belonging to each breed? I had a couple of spaniels here over the weekend and the difference between them and the Border Collies is quite remarkable.
22. How healthy is your dog? Have you been to the vet? How many of those visits were your fault? Did your puppy eat something they should not have done? Were any of these visits dues to breed or breeding issues? So far, Quin has not been to the vet (other than for his vaccinations).
23. Is your puppy what you expected? If not, why not? Have you had support from your breeder? Have you been in touch with the owners of your puppy's siblings? Each of my litters has a WhatsApp group, so they can share problems and celebrate successes!
24. Are you happy with way your dog was bred? Do you think they were given the best start in life? I have learnt that it makes a difference. A puppy that is cuddled every day likes being cuddled. It's that simple.
25. Is there anything about getting your puppy that you would do differently?

What still needs work?

I know that the current problems with Quin's recall are only temporary. He probably won't wreck much more around the house, if I pay him attention! But I need to work on his barking at other dogs, as this is irritating and can be fixed.

Weekly Focus Challenge

Please take a moment to reflect on your successes and the remaining challenges? Think about what you'd like to do with your dog in the next 6 months? Please do get in touch if you'd like to share any of the answers to my questions?

Share a picture of your dog. Write about how you got on with the challenge below.

_____

_____

_____

_____

_____

_____

WEEK 27: BOREDOM FIGHTING – PROBLEM

When your puppy is bored

I find the week between Christmas and New Year boring at the best of times, so it seems a good time to write about how to tackle a bored dog. I feel I am going over the same ground as I talked about a few weeks ago when I explained about punishing your dog, followed by the post about the disobedient puppy.

The purpose of this post is to stress that dogs do get bored if they are not correctly cared for. That boredom will inevitably appear as destructive behaviour, which will then lead to punishment and ultimately, re-homing. That's no good for anyone, so let's focus on tackling boredom in our puppy?

How much physical activity does a dog need?

This is like saying how long is piece of string, because not surprisingly dogs need different amounts of exercise and stimulation. Big dogs need not too much walking (bad for their joints) while little dogs need not too much walking (they only have little legs). NB: No puppy needs *loads* of exercise, but at 8 months old they are fine with an hour or so, if they are fit and healthy.

Walking your dog is NOT the way to stop boredom! If you walk a dog for hours every day what do you get? A fit dog (I typed 'git' dog – you'll get that too :p) And if you walk your dog on lead you *absolutely* won't solve the boredom. If anything, you'll make it worse, by increasing their frustration. What you cannot do is 'tire out' your dog. No way.

A dog needs to sniff and wander. It needs to move at its own pace, exploring and running around. Dogs do NOT travel in straight lines! Any attempt by you to keep your dog moving with you is detrimental to the dog's stimulation. Less stimulation means more boredom. An interesting walk, with plenty of sniffing, in a range of different environments (woods, fields, parks, beach) will tire out your dog. It will also make them calmer.

What else is an activity for a dog?

Apart from walking your dog, off lead, there are plenty of other ways to provide stimulation and enjoyment. Playing is obviously the main way you can entertain your dog. Ideally, they should be able to play on their own, or with your other dogs (I recommend having 5 dogs for this). Quin brings me toys for him to tug. It's a great game for him and relatively easy for me to do while reading a book, or watching TV. Tug, tug, tug. The girls prefer to bring toys to be thrown. Ounce loves to be thrown a toy, with the challenge being not to let her jump to catch it, or throw it where it causes accidents to furniture or other people or dogs.

Aura likes to watch Ounce's ball or toy being thrown, then try to get it before she does. Ounce will then either take it out of her mouth or tell her to drop it, which she instantly does. That's their game. You do have to watch that Aura doesn't sneak off with a toy, as she will then eat it, which the others rarely do.

Busy loves a shaky, snakey toy. Shake it! She does like you to throw it for her, but if you're busy with the others she'll just play with it herself. Running around, shaking her toy. Funny girl. **Dog toys** do not need to be expensive. You can use plastic bottles, flower pots, or bits of old jeans plaited together to make toys.

Chewing stops boredom

Hmm, well we don't want our dogs to chew, do we? Well yes, if they have the right thing to chew. Mine have **filled bones**, which last for months, even years. These are natural treats and really help to keep your dog occupied. You can buy lots of alternatives to these, such as **antlers, buffalo horn, chicken feet** etc. All pretty yucky if you're vegan, but dogs love them.

NB: Antlers are very hard and can break dogs' teeth. Luna broke a canine tooth on one, which had to be removed by the vet. Ouch!

There are other food related boredom busters. Kongs are an obvious one, but there are also licky mats and **snuffle mats**. All these require a bit of input from you to set these up, but can last for hours.

Training to fight boredom

Ultimately, your dog will be happiest and most relaxed if you spend time with him. When you hang out with your dog and better still, when you engage with your dog, they will not get bored and look for other entertainment. Just making a fuss of them, stroking and talking to them, will make them perfectly calm and content.

Training your dog is an even better way to provide stimulation for your dog. This might be a few tricks, or just a bit of 'work' whilst you are out on your walk. Perhaps a practice wait, or a down, or a bit of heelwork? You might also try out some other **activities, which will be discussed later.**

Finally – a word of warning

Please, please don't overdo it? Dogs sleep for around 12 hours a day, which means they should be asleep for large chunks of the day. Having that 'down time' is absolutely vital for their wellbeing. If your dog lives in a busy household, with lots of comings and goings, please try to make sure they have a quiet space to go to and are left alone for long periods?

Weekly Focus Challenge

How do you keep your dog entertained? What activities do you do? What do you plan to do with them in future? What problems have you had because your dog has been bored? Do you think you could manage this differently in future?

Share a picture of your dog. Write about how you got on with the challenge below.

_____

_____

_____

_____

_____

_____

WEEK 28: CRATES – INFORMATION

Why a dog crate is essential for your puppy

I am still using Quin's crate for him to sleep in, so I am reviewing why this is such an essential piece of equipment for your puppy. There are people who say 'I would never put my puppy in a cage!' That's lovely for them, as long as they are able to watch over their puppy 100% of the time and don't mind a few vet visits when the puppy eats a sock or other undesirable item. For most people though, a cage, or crate represents an easy way of keeping your puppy safe.

Keep your puppy safe

Someone once commented that you wouldn't put a baby in a crate. Well dur – what is a cot? Looks like a crate to me! We used to put children in playpens and I'm sure plenty of parents still use these. A dog crate is nothing more than a means to keep your puppy out of harm's way. You can't be watching your dog at all times and nor should you. Having the ability to pop them away safely for a while is common sense.

Having said that, you should not be using a crate at all times. My dogs sleep in their crates for 8 hours, but I wouldn't ever leave them in a crate during the day for more than a couple of hours. They have been absolutely fine in the van for 8 hours travelling up and down the country, just being let out once or twice to toilet. But I wouldn't especially do that all day, every day. Dogs who spend lots of time in crates can become bored and frustrated, which may lead to them being more anxious or guarding.

A safe space for your dog

Believe it or not, your dog loves to have its own quiet corner. Wild dogs will make a nest or bed in a ditch or under a bush. Dogs about to give birth will find a dark corner to nest in, away from the hustle and bustle of the house.

Set up your crate to be an enclosed, dark space, with a cover over most of the outside. I have seen people sharing horror stories of dogs becoming tangled in the covers or eating them, but I'm sure your dog will be fine if you use large blankets or towels to cover the crate and fold it neatly, so that only flat surfaces are facing the insides of the crate.

I always use vetbed inside. It's soft and fluffy, but is extremely lightweight and easy to wash. It is absorbent so if your dog has an accident, they will not be uncomfortable. If they are wet after a walk and then have to be left, they won't get cold. Vetbed is also durable so less likely to be chewed than standard pet beds.

How to train your dog to enjoy its crate

When I get a puppy, I feed them in their crate. Then, quietly close the door. Puppies love to search and sniff for pieces of food, and once they have found and eaten everything, they often settle down and drift into sleep for an hour or so. This gives you a chance to do other things without worrying about what the puppy is up to, and it is a good experience for the puppy to curl up and sleep in the crate by choice. You can gradually increase the time the puppy stays in the crate and initially this should be whilst you are in the room with it.

I try to have my puppy sleep in its crate from day one, but sometimes they need a bit of reassurance from you to start with. It's useful to say 'in your bed' when you want them to go in there.

NB: Always reward your dog for going into its crate. If you are going to leave them in there, make sure they have been to the toilet first, then give them a treat for going in, as well as some verbal praise.

And please:
- Never shout at your dog to go into its crate.
- Never drag your dog by the collar and shove it into the crate.
- Never allow children to get into the crate, with or without the dog
- Never take food or toys off your dog, especially when they are in their crate.

When to put the crate away

Most people long to pack their crate away, because it takes up space. I usually find that by six months your puppy should be reliably house trained and have stopped chewing most of the time. Or at least they are better at only chewing the things you give them! However, if your dog is happy to sleep in the crate, I would leave it up, if you can. They are safe and they feel safe.

Weekly Focus Challenge

Where does your dog sleep? If you have a crate, how have you found it? Does your dog like sleeping in it? How much time do they spend in it? Do you reward them every time they go in it? When do/did you take it away? Have you had any issues since then?

Share a picture of your dog. Write about how you got on with the challenge below.

WEEK 29: TRICKS – TRAINING

Tricks to entertain you and your puppy

Teaching your puppy to do something counts as a trick. You give the word and they do as you ask – hurray! So it could be as simple as getting your dog into a sit, or a down. Anything which gives you a bit more control when you need it is useful to have.

Taking it to the next level is a way of engaging with your dog and making sure that they listen to you. It is also a great way of giving your dog rewards for paying attention. This will keep your dog stimulated and ultimately happy. It's incidentally a brilliant thing to have up your sleeve for when it's raining, or you're bored, or you can't walk your dog because of illness, either in your dog or in you.

Getting started with tricks training

Before attending a class, you need to consider if you will be bothered to work on any of the tricks. You might feel that your dog is fine just mooching around the house and having a bit of petting and love from you. That's absolutely fine.
If you want a bit more from your dog, start by teaching simple commands like 'sit' and 'wait'.

Or you could teach a 'down'. Recall is also part of basic training for any dog. There are quite a few tricks that are useful for a dog to have. Just being handled and coping with you or someone else, such as a vet or groomer touching your dog can become something that you need to work on.

Some tricks are more interesting for the dog to do or just more entertaining for you to have. On the website I shared the video of Ounce opening the door of her crate and going inside. Clever girl!

Luring vs Shaping

When Quin and I went to our first 'Trickstars' training class, the excellent Nicola Smith from Lucky Dog Training started by talking about the difference between luring and shaping. Luring is when you use your hand, holding food, to show your dog what you want. You put the food on the end of his nose and move it slowly where you want him to go. This is easy to do and produces good results. Great, you think, I've taught my dog to sit, or go into a down. That was quick!

Unfortunately, your dog has not learnt to do those things. They have learned to follow your hand in order to get the treat. If you remove your hand, or even if you just remove the treat, your dog will struggle to do what you want. It's quite hard for your dog to understand what you want and they probably weren't paying much attention to you when there was food at the end of their nose.

Wait for it...

Shaping is when you wait for your dog to offer you the right behaviour. When it works, it's like magic! So how do you make it work? You wait for it. It's much more difficult to do. The dog must be 'set up to succeed'. So when I talked about training your dog to **fetch a toy**, I said you needed to reward your dog for going near the toy, or sniffing it. This is shaping the behaviour of your dog. You are encouraging the dog to think about what gets the reward and to allow them to process that.

You can start shaping by putting down an obstacle and seeing what the dog will do to get a treat. That's the first thing we tackled in our **class** yesterday. Or you can do what I do, eat a bag of crisps and wait for your dogs to offer something to get one. Ounce has quite the repertoire! She will twist, go down, sit, give a paw and speak (loudly). Give me a crisp mum!

Clicker training

Lots of dog trainers use a clicker to mark the behaviour that they are looking for in the dog. A **clicker** makes a noise when pressed, which you can do at the exact second your dog does what you like. You then give them a reward. The only problem with a clicker is that you need lots of hands! You need to hold the clicker and make it work, hold the treats and give them to your dog, hold your dog's lead, or toy, or show your dog what you want. It's a lot to manage! An alternative to a clicker is to replace it with a word, or a tongue click. Most people use 'Yes!' as it is quick to say, has a distinct sound and is rewarding for you as well as the dog!

Simple tricks to try

I recommend using a trainer like Nicola and **following a course** or attending a class. It's quite intense going to a two hour workshop, but a good trainer will break it down and teach a variety of tricks during the session, with a break halfway through.   The tricks we covered yesterday included:

- Paws onto step, back feet on floor
- Nose touch to hand
- Card touch as a starting point to teach touching something on a wall
- Turn around bowl – going on from the first one but moving back legs around in a circle
- Nose into cone, to start hiding their face
- Bow, like the play bow dogs do
- Head down on the floor when they are lying down
- Pick up duster – tidy up!

Quin was brilliantly behaved and managed to keep going even though it was hard work. He finished off with a real highlight. He is used to getting objects and bringing them to me, so immediately grabbed the duster and brought it to me. I was then offering his tuggy to play, as he'd had so many treats. This made him drop the duster, so Nicola then placed a box underneath and he dropped in on that. Tidying up! It was a fantastic end to a great session.

Weekly Focus Challenge

What tricks can your dog do so far? Do you fancy learning anything else? It's great to have a 'party piece' so I recommend picking one or two things to try teaching your dog.

Share a picture of your dog. Write about how you got on with the challenge below.

WEEK 30: REVIEW THE PROBLEMS – PROBLEM

What are the problems you have with your puppy?

Puppy problems can be hard to tackle, but we don't necessarily have to solve every problem. At this age, we may feel that we have our finished dog. They are adult-sized and we have had them for a long time. Unfortunately, it's not quite that simple. We still have work to do, if we want to get the finished dog we dreamed of having.

Hopefully when you read through my questionnaire celebrating six months with your puppy, you thought about what was really great about them? And what was not so great? Did you find yourself realising that there are things you are not entirely happy with? I know I did. Quin is so lovely around the house and when he meets people. He is not so great with other dogs and this is the area that needs thinking about.

Defining the puppy problems

When you think about your dog, what problems spring to mind? The most common puppy problems around the ages of 6-10 months are:

- Excessive barking in the house and garden
- Barking at and chasing cats, squirrels and birds
- Barking at the door/when visitors arrive
- Jumping up
- Pulling on the lead
- Not coming back (recall)
- Reacting to other dogs on walks
- Chasing cars/runners/bikes
- Chewing the furniture/shoes/the house
- Needing too much exercise/being too lively

Sound familiar? These problems are *really common!* So first of all, recognise that you have a dog and that's what dogs do? Hopefully, some of these problems are ones you have already tackled, with me. Search the website to see the posts I have already written about these issues?

Decide what to do

You have recognised your dog's biggest issues. Now decide what you want to do? You have three choices:

- Do nothing
- Manage it
- Train it away

First of all, don't underestimate the decision to do nothing. You have a dog. Some things that you find really annoying are just part of who your dog is. You might just need to accept that and cope with it. Barking is the biggest of these types of puppy problems.

Do nothing

Quin barks at lots of things, including animals (especially dogs!) on the TV. It's hilarious. Most dogs don't react to the TV, or only look round if a dog barks. Quin leaps up and stares at the screen if a chicken appears! He is very fierce and gets really annoyed if we watch a wildlife programme. Funny boy. We don't really mind, we just call him to distract him and give him a fuss once he stops barking. It's fine, he'll probably grow out of it.

One of the posts I've linked to on the website shows my efforts to stop Aura going berserk when the food processor is switched on. However, it doesn't really bother us when the dogs all go mad occasionally, so I don't keep revisiting this training.

Manage it

Barking around the house can be managed relatively easily, by putting the dog away from the source of the stimulation. So when someone comes to the door, put the dog in another room so they don't get rewarded by the door being answered. You're pretty unlikely to stop them barking altogether, but at least they are not rewarded for barking.

The most common issues that people choose to manage are pulling on lead and not coming back. People use harnesses with their dogs so that when they pull on lead they don't strangle themselves. That's fine if you don't mind being pulled along. It's actually useful if you are doing Canicross!

When dogs don't come straight back to their owners, the owners get scared their dog will get run over, or that they will be attacked by another dog. So they keep them on lead. Some owners don't even try to let their dogs off lead.

For me personally, I think it's absolutely tragic if you choose not to tackle either of these issues. In my opinion (humble or otherwise), it is absolutely essential for dogs to walk off lead. Therefore they don't necessarily need a **harness** if they don't walk far on lead, but it's obviously better if they can walk sensibly. And it's vital for a dog to be able to wander and sniff, at their own pace.

Train it away

By far the best solution, for you and the dog, is to put in a bit of work to make puppy problems more manageable. **WARNING: Some problems are more easily solved than others!** **Jumping up** is a relatively simple problem to solve, whereas **reacting to other dogs** and **not coming back** when called are worthy of several blog posts on their own.

Hopefully though, this post has encouraged you to think about the ongoing issues with your problem puppy and make a plan about what you want to fix, what you are able to manage and what you can just ignore? I am working hard with Quin to help him cope with meeting other dogs – more on this in the coming weeks.

Weekly Focus Challenge

What does your dog do that drives you mad? How are you going to tackle each of their problems? Make a list of the problems and then decide how you are going to cope with them.

Share a picture of your dog being good. Write about how you got on with the challenge below.

WEEK 31: FOOD – INFORMATION

Dog food – what is best for your dog?

The dog food market is absolutely enormous; it's worth billions of pounds. So we are all subject to huge commercial pressure to buy certain types of food for our dog. When I was young the choice was between two or three types of tinned meat, plus a biscuit meal to add bulk. Even longer ago, dogs were simply fed scraps and leftovers – dog food didn't exist.

Today we are bombarded with choice over different types of dog food and we now consider there to be four main ways we can feed our dogs:

- dry complete food, or kibble
- wet tinned food
- home cooked food
- raw food.

There is a huge amount of information available now about what type of dog food is best for your dog. I am not a nutritionist, so I am not going to wade into this argument. I am simply going to highlight a few of the **issues and questions around dog food**, as I have done previously.

Dog food – fit for your dog

Dogs come in all shapes and sizes! They also live very different lives – from a toy dog, such as a Yorkshire Terrier, living in a city and being carried around, to **Border Collie**, working sheep in the hills. Clearly the needs of those two animals will be very different. So I think you need to start by examining your dog's size and shape and considering their level of activity and fitness.

A good starting point with dog food is to talk to the breeder. **Responsible breeders** will have experience of the breed and what works well for them. That doesn't mean you have to feed the same food, just that they have tried out different foods and worked out what works for them. As a **Kennel Club Assured Breeder**, I am required to provide advice about feeding to my puppy owners. I also provide a few days of puppy food and offer a sack of food at a discounted price.

Monitor your dog

When you get your puppy, you need to assess whether the food they have is working for them. Are they too fat, or too thin? Is their level of activity correct for the life they are living? I have seen dogs that are lacking in energy and struggling to enjoy the same walks that my dogs do. Equally, I have seen dogs that are 'wired', leaping around all over the house, struggling to settle.

Think about the what you need your dog to do? Hopefully you will keep their routine similar on a day-to-day basis. If you are going to go on a long hike, you need to think about giving your dog a bigger breakfast before you go and perhaps taking a small meal for them to have at lunchtime, while you are in the pub!

If you are going to run around with your dog, doing **agility** for example, you need to feed them early enough so that this is digested. Don't feed immediately after exercise either, as this can lead to bloating, which is a serious medical condition.

Quality of poo

Well if you own a dog, you will come face to face with this issue on a daily basis! We have to pick up after our dogs, so we do become invested in what is coming out of them. A dog with an upset stomach is not nice for them or you. **Border Collies** are notoriously fussy, picky eaters. They certainly don't eat everything! As a breed, they often have digestive issues and are quite sensitive to different foods. They are by no means the only breed to suffer in this way – poodles are quite sensitive to allergies, which obviously can affect poodle crossbreeds as well.

Tailor-made dog food

For me, I like a nice complete food that is easy to feed. I was recommended to feed **Royal Canin** when I started breeding and it works for me. That doesn't mean I feed it indiscriminately to my dogs.

Luna has a diabetic version which helps maintains her health really well, despite her diabetes. I obviously feed the younger dogs a version for puppies and junior dogs, while the older dogs have a senior version.

In addition I add extra bits for interest. One of the main criticisms of feeding kibble is that it's boring. Personally, that is not an issue for me, as I have bran flakes for my breakfast every single day. I like it, it's easy and I don't see why I have to have variety for breakfast. Again, the amount of variety your dog wants will vary from one dog to the next.

Raw feeding

In my opinion, **feeding raw meat to dogs** is fraught with difficulties. It's harder to manage from a hygiene point of view – see the **government's handling guidelines**. The reason I don't routinely feed it to my dogs is because they're not bothered about it. It's certainly not their favourite.

I have tried feeding my dogs **Aardvark** kibble containing insect protein. I love the idea of replacing meat with insects in our food. Again, the dogs weren't that fussed. So I stick to what they eat, what keeps them the right weight and fitness. I add raw carrot and goat's milk powder for a bit of extra tastiness. Lucky dogs!

Meat and vegetables

Dogs are omnivores and need to eat a range of foods, not just meat. All commercially produced kibble contains a mix of food sources. There is a lot of criticism of these, with people believing that a 'grain-free' diet is better for their dogs. The evidence does not support that, with actual allergies to wheat etc being very rare.

Changing foods

If you decide to change your dog's food, make sure you do this gradually. Mix it in with the old food and slowly change the ratio of old to new, over a few days. Ideally, ask friends or your breeder what foods they recommend and perhaps get a week's supply from them? Then you are not committing to a whole sack that they then refuse to eat. If they don't really like a new food, mix it in with the old food to use it up.

Popular brands

Finally, please don't think you can just buy the supermarket own brand, or worse still, the popular brand beginning with B! (It rhymes with Fakers) This brand is full of colours and preservatives, not with balanced ingredients we want to feed our dogs.

Weekly Focus Challenge

Are you happy with the weight and condition of your dog? Do you think they are 'fit for purpose'? Do they like their food or do you feel they are not that bothered? If you have a very hungry dog, you may need to consider something different. Or if they wolf their food down too quickly, you may want to feed them differently, using a snuffle mat, for example (see boredom fighting).

Share a picture of your dog being good. Write about any problems or successes relating to their food.

WEEK 32: RECALL AGAIN – TRAINING

How's your recall going?

Recall is the hardest 'skill' to master when you have a dog – and the most important. I have already talked about calling your puppy several times during the course of writing this book and elsewhere on the website. But it is so important it is worth revisiting and revising. Having just re-read the last chapter I wrote about recall, I don't have much to add. I'm just putting this here to remind you to keep on practising.

Test yourself with these challenges:

- Call your dog 5 times in the house, when you can see them. How quickly do they respond?
- Call your dog 5 times from another room. Do they still come?
- Call your dog 5 times from the garden. If you are inside and they are outside, do they still come back? Or do you normally just wait until they have 'finished' being in the garden and come in on their own?
- Call your dog 5 times on your walk. Now what happens?

Why does recall work?

Think about the difference in the way your dog responds to you. What makes your recall successful? What stops your dog from coming back to you? What's the quickest you can get your dog back to you?

I have previously mentioned having a 'Pavlovian response' to recall and I think this is at the heart of making it work for you and your puppy. What you need to do is create a situation where your dog has *a very strong association between you calling their name and them receiving a reward*. Once you have that, it is very difficult for the dog to ignore you.

Remember, your dog is not malicious. They don't spend their time imagining ways to wind you up, or annoy you. Dogs want an easy, happy life. If you feed them tasty treats and play with them, they want to be with you.

Instant recall

How quickly do you need your dog back? Do you absolutely have to have them under control at all times? I urge you to be realistic and manage your expectations with regard to recall. If your dog is having a good old sniff, or has wandered off a bit in the woods to see if a squirrel is there to be chased, please be patient?

If your dog is rushing over to another dog, you need to weigh up the impact of that encounter. When you know that your dog is relaxed and happy meeting other dogs, you don't need to panic, but you do still need to call them and pay attention to the meeting. If your dog is currently being a bit of a dick when seeing other dogs (like Quin) you need a sharper and more persistent recall. More on that later..

Breed variations in recall

Of course there are very specific breed characteristics that massively affect the quality of a dog's recall. **Border Collies** have a strong desire to please, which means they will 'work' for a reward. However, they do run fast and far. They also have a keen eye, so if they spot something, they may well shoot off. Fortunately, they are pretty snappy to respond, even when they are heading off.

Other breeds are tricky for different reasons. Hounds and Gundogs are 100% scent driven and when they get a whiff of something interesting, can be *extremely* hard to turn around. Now that I am doing some scentwork training though, I feel that the smell of cheese, sausage or liver cake will carry quite a distance to a well-conditioned dog!

Some dogs, such as Toy breeds, are a bit slower to respond, because they are well, slower to respond. Training them is harder because they are more laid back and less focused. Patience is required! And practice, always.

Let it fail

Nobody's perfect. Well I'm certainly not. Try to be kind to yourself and your dog? It won't go perfectly every time, but if you keep practising, it WILL get better. I've definitely seen an improvement in Quin's recall over the past couple of weeks. He was going through a phase of not being that bothered about coming back to me, especially if he was barking at another dog. That is getting better and he really is returning to me now – hurray! But there are still plenty of times when it's not that great.

Remember the key rules for recall:

- reward
- practice
- reward
- be positive
- reward

Weekly Focus Challenge

Try the recall challenge? How did you get on? Think about how much you practice your recall. Do you need to do more? Do you remember to take treats with you on your walks? What do you think you need to do better?

Share a picture of your dog coming back. Write about how you got on with the challenge below.

_____
_____
_____
_____
_____
_____
_____

WEEK 33: REACTIVITY – PROBLEM

Reactivity is such a challenge

How do you cope when your dog is reactive to certain situations? **Reactivity** is the worst problem we have to deal with in our dogs and for some people, very hard to cope with. Many owners sadly feel unable to train their dog past this and that is such a shame. Let's start with a definition:

*"Reactivity is commonly confused with aggression. Dogs that **are reactive overreact to certain stimuli or situations**. Genetics, lack of socialization, insufficient training to learn self-control, a frightening experience, or a combination of these can cause reactivity, and fear is typically the driving force."*

What are dogs reactive to?

Reactivity results in manic barking and this can be at all sorts of things, including:

- other dogs
- runners
- cyclists
- cars
- people

Remember, there are **different types of barking** and these are not all reactivity. Reactivity is when a dog is afraid, as described in the definition above. At other times the dog may just be excited! Start by learning about your dog's different kinds of barking and whether they are really demonstrating reactivity.

How to tackle reactivity

I feel reasonably confident talking about this issue now, having had a dog who was pretty reactive. Quin has been barking very loudly at lots of dogs we have gone past on walks. I've found it really hard work to deal with and knowing how to tackle it. I have thought about putting him on lead more, or even buying a **basket muzzle** for him to wear, in case he went for other dogs. Fortunately, I decided to work through it. Here are my tips.

Start by staying calm. You will not help your dog by 'reacting' yourself. Hopefully, you have a **brilliant recall**, or your dog is already on lead. Call your dog to get its attention, calmly and quietly. When your dog is focused on you, albeit they may still be looking at the 'disturbance', give quiet praise.

My friend Kate from the The Canine Hub recommends saying 'Nice!' whilst rewarding, as it keeps everything calmer. That's it. Calm, focus, distraction. The trick though is to be aware of what may cause a stimulation and a reaction and be ready to tackle it. I've come unstuck a few times when the dogs have been running ahead of me and another dog has suddenly appeared round a corner. Not surprisingly, Quin has been a bit wary and has reacted by barking.

Warning: Don't come near me!

This is what your dog is saying. They are also saying 'help me!' Your dog is not sure what is happening and wants you to support them. They are also warning you that something might be a danger and they can easily turn this into a compulsion to guard you. How they learn to cope really does depend on how you tackle it. If you grip your dog's lead, shout at them to be quiet and drag them away, the dog learns that barking is just what is needed.

One step at a time

Like so many areas of training your dog, reactivity is something best tackled one step at a time. You won't fix it in one day, but need to persevere. As I said at the start of this post, I could have just put Quin on the lead on walks, or bunged a muzzle on him and dragged him past other dogs. Instead, I have chosen to work through this problem. Here are some of the steps I have taken:

- practise recall, many times a day
- practise saying 'nice' when I have his attention, with gentle stroking
- walk with friends and their dogs, to ensure he has plenty of interaction without reaction
- stop and chat to people when he has reacted to their dog. This has made him calm down and he has been able to wander off, then come back to me for a fuss
- grab hold of him as people are coming towards me and calmly hold him still, stroking and praising – nice!
- pop him on lead or hold his collar whilst going past some people

Result!

In the last few days, as we go towards other dogs, Quin has been able to turn and look at me, then come back for a quick cuddle (and a sweetie!) then go past the other dogs, just like the girls do. Hurray! This is so magical for me, as honestly, a couple of weeks ago he was barking so violently, right in dogs' faces! Of course I realise he will bark again – we haven't stopped it permanently. I am sure I will forget to pay attention and another dog will rush up to him barking, which will set him back a bit. But that's fine. It's a work in progress. Other dogs are learning at their own pace. Quin will also have other problem I will need to tackle…

Be kind

It is absolutely infuriating when other dogs rush over to yours and bark in their face. I can completely understand why people become enraged and shout at the other dog owner. 'Control your dog!' Please try to be kind though when this happens. If we don't let our dogs off lead, they can't learn to behave themselves. And if we don't try and fix it, it won't be fixed, will it? Please don't shout at the other person or their dog unless they are showing *no attempt* to recall them? If the other person is making an effort, try to be patient with them? Recall your dog and reward them for being brilliant!

Weekly Focus Challenge

How reactive is your dog? What do they struggle to cope with? How do you manage this? Do you think the problem is getting better, or worse?

Share a picture of your dog being happy and relaxed. Write about how you got on with the challenge below.

WEEK 34: NEUTERING – INFORMATION

Neutering your dog – the pros and cons

Quin tried to hump his Auntie Luna this morning, so this seems likely a timely post! Neutering is not a simple issue and as with so many aspects of dog ownership, it is subject to fashion and cultural context. When I was growing up, I don't think neutering in dogs was done routinely; it was more often carried out when a dog was becoming a problem. Male dogs were often allowed to roam the streets, looking for a mate and puppies were very often produced through a neighbour's dog appearing in a garden one day.

Of course these things do still happen, but happily we are inching forwards to a culture where responsible dog ownership is becoming more commonplace. There has been a view that dogs were who were not 'entire' would be affected in their personality; that this would be detrimental to their character. Increasingly, I am of the view that any changes are positive, especially to male dogs.

Most recently, there has been a movement to 'protect a dog's rights'; it is illegal to neuter dogs and cats in Norway without good medical reason. However, there is plenty of evidence for **good medical reasons**.

Freedom to roam

In the past, dog owners who were being responsible would whip their puppy off to the vet's to be neutered almost as soon as they were brought home. When I got my first puppy, in 1987, the expectation was that he would be castrated at six months, so that his behaviour would remain more manageable. He still cocked his leg and enjoyed playing around with Sunny when she was in season, but he didn't hump your leg, (which was good!) and he didn't try to go off roaming the neighbourhood.

More recently, we are finding that it is good to allow dogs to reach full maturity before they are neutered, both male and female. If you search online, you will find articles such as this one from the Blue Cross about **neutering your dog**. This says that there are a number of health benefits to neutering early, such as reducing the chances of cancers.

However, another article cites the benefits of neutering later:

"When a dog's testes or ovaries are removed, the production of hormones is interrupted, which affects bone growth. Because the bone growth plates may close earlier in dogs neutered young, orthopaedic problems such as hip dysplasia and cranial cruciate ligament tears may result. Neutered dogs also tend to gain excess weight, further stressing the joints. But neutering does not equal obesity. It's more difficult to keep neutered dogs in shape, but it can be done."

Personally, I think it does come down to good management. If you feel that you will struggle to cope with an unneutered dog, get it done from the age of six months. You might be able to manage for a while, so you can leave it until the dog has reached maturity, which for collies would be around a year to 18 months. However, if you can't be bothered with the hassle, definitely get them neutered.

Coming into season

Elsewhere, I have written about what happens to a bitch coming into season and how to manage this. If you are prepared for the need to pay attention to your dog every 6-8 months and make sure that they do not come into contact with uncastrated dogs, then you may choose to leave your dog unneutered.

As I said earlier, I had my previous male dog, Buzz castrated at the age of six months. My first bitch, Rue was done in middle age, having had two litters of pups. Much safer to have the operation, I thought at the time. I had planned to have Sunny spayed once she had had her third litter, but I hesitated because I felt that it was a major operation that she did not need to have.

Neutering – emergency procedures

I wrote about this subject a few years ago, having brought Sunny home from the vet. She had an emergency spay, aged 12 years, following pyometra, or pyo.
"Pyometra is defined as an infection in the uterus. Pyometra is considered a serious and life threatening condition that must be treated quickly and aggressively."

Symptoms of Pyometra include:

- Abdominal distention (from an enlarged uterus)
- Vulvar (vaginal) discharge
- Closed cervix
- Lethargy

- Depression
- Lack of appetite
- Vomiting
- Frequent urination.

Fortunately for us, Sunny's condition was picked up quickly by me and surgery was straightforward. She stayed in overnight for observation, but she recovered remarkably quickly. However, I can't understate the anxiety I have with all my 'entire' girls as they come into season and out again.

Other emergencies and health issues

Sadly, Luna had to have a Caesarean with her last litter and when the vet asked if I wanted her spayed as well, I thought 'why not'. I asked if it would make the operation more complicated and he said "No, it will be simpler, as it's easier to remove everything." I then didn't have to worry about post-op infection in her uterus as it had all been taken out!

Luna made such a great recovery from the operation and really rocked the shirt provided by the vet, which was brilliant compared with the stupid lampshade they usually provide. She was moving around normally within a day or two and a month today since the op she if fully healed and back to her usual self.

JB also had to be neutered, following a urine infection that just wouldn't clear, leading to prostatitis. There are so many issues that can affect a dog's health, unfortunately.

Quick recoveries

On the strength of that, I decided to go ahead with Aura's spay. Aura is more active than Luna, so I thought it might be harder to manage her recovery. Silly me! She is younger and fitter than her mum, so was completely better within the week. Amazing. Busy was the same.

Now I don't have to worry about them being in season when I enter shows and I have less girls to clear up after. No more worrying about dogs chasing us when we are out – at least with these three. I am a total convert. And of course now I have another boy, I don't want a funny family business going on! Quin will still need careful management in future.

In conclusion

In my opinion, the recommendation I give my puppy owners is this: Leave it until they reach maturity, so that their bones have a chance to develop fully and normally. Then do it! Stop the production of unwanted dogs and make your life easier. Then make sure you keep your dog fit and healthy, through exercise and training.

Weekly Focus Challenge

When do you plan to get your dog neutered? What does your vet think about it? You should respect their views and experience, whilst being mindful of what is best for your dog and your situation. You certainly shouldn't breed from your dog, unless you are a very experienced dog owner, with a good understanding of the issues involved.

Share a picture of your dog. Write about how you got on with the challenge below.

WEEK 35: SOCIALISING ON WALKS – TRAINING

Socialising on walks

I've talked about **socialising** on a few occasions, but today I am focusing on walking with friends, by meeting up and going on a walk together. I am fortunate to have plenty of 'dog friends' these days and I enjoy nothing better than to meet up for a walk and a catch up. This is a different thing from meeting people on a walk and stopping for a chat, or even walking along with someone you see on a walk.

Allowing your dog to meet and spend time around other dogs is such a great thing to do. So many people struggle with **socialising** their dogs, which stops them from being able to let their dogs off lead and run around.

What difference does it make to your dog?

Well believe it or not, dogs do have friends, just like us. If they see another dog regularly, they can get to know them and build up their confidence in running and playing together. Sometimes it takes a while for dogs to get to know each other, but most dogs like to see the same dogs and have the chance to walk along together. When I meet up with friends, I find that if we just set off together, the dogs will set off with us. If we have to start on lead, that's fine, they can walk slightly apart, but moving forward. Then you let them off and away they go!

The main benefits

Dogs on a pack walk will usually be more active, running around more and following each other about. They should also be more engaged, sniffing what the other dogs sniff and of course toileting, or marking where the other dogs have been!

I think it is really important to share your experiences of your dog with like-minded people. The main benefit of going to training classes, in my view, is not just for **socialisation for your dog**, but for the socialisation for you! In a class situation, it can be tricky to let the dogs socialise properly, as you have a job to do. Walking provides a much better situation for everyone to get along.

Possible problems

There are a few possible problems with **socialising** on a walk. First of all, the dogs need to meet and get along. As I've said, it's better to just get walking. Standing chatting is when problems are more likely to occur. Move forward and the dogs will get on with it. You might find they don't seem to interact that much – it's fine. They are sharing the experience and if you walk together fairly often, they will definitely enjoy being together.

Other problems can occur if one gets a scent and takes the others off with it. You may well find that recall is harder when other dogs are around. The trick with this is to coordinate your efforts. When one of you calls your dog, get the others to also call their dogs. Then it all becomes interesting and exciting for the dogs! If they really aren't listening, you will all have to try the 'running away' tactic.

You will definitely need more treats than usual! Or tastier ones, at least. But don't be too demanding of your dog? Manage your expectations; they are having fun and don't need you hassling them all the time! I do recommend calling them in for a treat and a fuss, with if possible a quick second or two on lead and then praise and off they go again.

When you have several young unneutered dogs of the same age and sex, don't be surprised if they have a bit of a scrap at some point? Usually, they will sort themselves out really quickly, but you may have to intervene. Ideally, they should be the same size, so there won't be any damage. Just be aware of the dynamic and be ready to interfere if necessary. A loud shout should be enough to break things up. Oh and keep counting. How many dogs do we have?

Weekly Focus Challenge

Do you walk with friends and their dogs? If you don't have any friends locally, try asking the people you meet on your walks if they would mind if you walk along with them for a while? Or join a group on social media and see if anyone wants to meet up?

Share a picture of your dog being good. Write about how you got on with the challenge below.

_____

_____

_____

_____

_____

_____

_____

WEEK 36: CAT CHASING – PROBLEM

Can your puppy live with cats?

Cats are lovely (not as nice as dogs, admittedly, but they have their place). I've had cats for most of my life and for large chunks of that time they have lived perfectly successfully alongside dogs. It can be a problem though, if your dog pesters the cat, or chases it. So how can we manage this?

Why do dogs chase cats?

I don't believe it takes a rocket scientist to answer this question does it? Cats are small enough to be 'prey'. But more importantly, they run away! Well, they might turn into a fierce monster first, becoming as giant as a tiger, but ultimately, if they're given a bit of a nudge, they usually run. Hurray! So much fun to be had!

Some cats are naturally better at ignoring dogs. Most people will have seen a cat confidently stalk through a group of dogs, casually ignoring them.

Can cats and dogs be friends?

I believe cats and dogs can be friends and that it enhances both their lives (and yours) if you can live together nicely. But is might take some work on your part! I think the starting point is to assume that any animal you introduce to the house will NOT get on with your other animals. They need time to settle into the environment first, before they are introduced to potentially hostile housemates. So I would always start by keeping dogs and cats well away from each other.

A means to escape

Once you do introduce them, make sure the cat can get to a high place, out of the way. Allow them to go there, where they can safely observe the stupid, annoying dog.

As always, be patient! Take your time and don't rush. I've had rescue dogs in the house with cats and they definitely are more of a challenge! You will need to manage them for longer and be more vigilant.

As usual, you will need to reward your dog for the behaviour you want around your cat. Wait until they look away, or sit down, or come to you and then give a positive 'Yes!' and a **treat**. You could try training your cat of course. Good luck with that!

NB: If you want a rescue dog, it is extremely unlikely you will be allowed to have one if you have cats. As I've said, it is much more difficult to manage an older dog. It can be done though.

Of course if you are out on a walk and your dog sees a cat, they will almost certainly try and chase it, even if they live with a cat. You'll just have to keep working on your **recall**...

Weekly Focus Challenge

How does your dog react to a cat? If you have a cat, do they live happily alongside your dog? How do you manage this? If you don't have a cat, what would you do if one came to stay?

Share a picture of your dog being good. Write about how you got on with the challenge below.

WEEK 37: GOING ON HOLIDAY – INFORMATION

Holidays with your dogs

In the old days, I rarely took my **dogs on holiday**. I have been lucky enough to travel abroad to quite a few countries and to have some fabulous holidays. These days things look different. We now enjoy travelling around the UK, which means we can take our dogs on holiday – hurray!

Having said that, I have taken my dogs away, but mainly to stay with family. Over the past few years I have been away with a few of my dogs, staying in hotels and self-catering accommodation. Nowadays I am confident enough to take all five away with me!

What do you need to think about?

There are various websites and **groups on social media**, advertising 'really REALLY dog friendly holidays'. Reading through the posts, the first consideration when booking something seems to be 'does it have a secure garden?'

First of all, the accommodation needs to be suitable for dogs. Some holiday companies will allow 'one or two small dogs', but nowadays there are plenty of 'proper' places advertising space for multiple dogs. I think it is perfectly possible to stay in a place for a week and leave it spotless, provided you are equipped to do so. This means taking beds, such as plenty of vetbed, together with throws and towels. If your dog goes on the sofa at home you won't keep them off it in the holiday place, will you?

A dog friendly area?

Apparently the most dog-friendly town in the UK is **Keswick**, in the Lake District. It is certainly beautiful. ALL the cafes let you bring dogs into them and there are plenty of fabulous walks. We stayed in a hotel, which was great, except there was NO place to toilet the dogs! So at 10.30pm I had to set off for a five-minute walk up the road to the park. Nightmare.

Lots of people want a beach to walk along, but not all beaches allow dogs, so do check before you go. If you do go on the beach a lot, make sure you wash your dogs off afterwards and dry them thoroughly, as the sand can be a real irritant.

Hiking

If you are going for a hike, make sure you take some water and travel bowl for your dog. Many hills and mountains have streams along the way, but you can't necessarily count on this. If you are walking across hills, be aware that if there are sheep around, you will need to keep your dog under control.

You might want to take snacks for your dog as well as for yourself. If your dog normally only walks for an hour and you suddenly do a 2-3 hour hike, they will be just as tired as you are. Especially if they are off lead and whizzing about exploring!

What to take away with you

When going on holiday with your dog, you need to be prepared. I keep a list on my phone, ready to help me pack.

Here are some of the items on my list:
- leads, including a couple of spares
- bowls, including water bowls
- food, measured out into bags
- medication
- beds, towels and throws
- toys, especially chews or bones, if they are going to be left in the car or accommodation
- cleaning kit
- plenty of waterproof and walking clothes and boots

NB: There is no such thing as bad weather, only bad clothing.

Weekly Focus Challenge

Can you take your puppy away with you? What would you have to think about? Where will you go? Think about what might make it possible.

Share a picture of your dog being good. Write about how you got on with the challenge below.

_____

_____

_____

_____

_____

_____

_____

WEEK 38: STOP THE DOG – TRAINING

Can your dog stop on command?

Being able to stop your dog when they are running away from you, or towards you, is extremely useful. However, I am realistic in thinking that this is easy to achieve, especially if you do NOT have a **Border Collie**!

One of the main reasons people don't let their dogs off lead is because they are sure that they will 'run off'. There are many reasons why a dog might run off, including:

- chasing after something, such as a squirrel, deer, rabbit or cat
- chasing a car
- being chased by another dog
- being frightened, usually by a loud bang from a firework, thunder or gunshot
- wandering off due to age and infirmity.

Obviously these reasons are all serious, challenging issues and can result in dogs getting lost. Fortunately, because it is now **a legal requirement for breeders to microchip their puppies** and for owners to transfer the details into their name, dogs are not lost for long. Once they get to a vet, they can be scanned and returned home.

Can you really stop a dog?

Honestly, not always. Many dogs have a very strong prey drive and will give chase to prey, once it is flushed. Dogs will do what they are bred for and you should not expect anything else. Equally, some dogs are easily spooked and will run off home, or hide in bushes.

I have heard of many stories of dogs running off, scared, only to be found hours later hiding in a bush beside where the car is normally parked. I remember Buzz being scared by a couple of German Shepherds when he was a pup. He ran off, I went home and then had to go off searching. Of course he came home, but obviously not the same way as me!

Worth a try

Despite these challenges, it's still worth thinking about being able to stop your dog. There are many, less scary situations where it is useful to be able to stop your dog. With several (well OK lots of) dogs, I sometimes find myself on one side of a road, with some of the dogs having crossed over. No cars when they went, but when I turn round to collect the last one, a car is coming. Help! Now I need to stop the others crossing back to me. I would usually stop the car and make sure we were all across, but it's amazing how easily things like that happen.

Of course you don't want to wait until you get into difficulties before you try to stop your dog. Give it a go while you are on the walk.

Start small

Wait until your dog is wandering away from you, then call out "Wait!" or "Stop!" See what they do? If they pause, even if they look back at you, say "Yes!" and then go over and give them a treat. Keep trying it and see if you can get a bit of distance, or a bit of speed, or both.

The next step is to try stopping the dog when it is coming towards you. I sometimes find putting my hand up helps to make the dog think about what you want.

Which command to use?

I work on teaching a down command, with distance, from an early age. 'Down' is one of the first things I teach my puppies, as it is so useful. I keep on using it until my dog can go down on a verbal command only. Once this is secure, I can add distance. I keep practising this until my dogs drop when I shout down, even when they are running around, either going away or coming towards me.

'Down' is probably easier to achieve than 'wait' when the dogs stands still, but again, it depends on the breed and their desire to please! Do NOT expect a sit. That won't help. Dogs don't really like sitting.

Whatever you do, keep practising, keep rewarding and keep engaging with your puppy!

Weekly Focus Challenge

Can you stop your dog? Try stopping them when they are moving away from you and when they are coming towards you. Try stopping them when they are just 'mooching' rather than running. Try it before they are looking at something else. The more you practice and the more you reward, the more likely you are going to be able to stop them when it really matters. Good luck!

Share a picture of your dog being good. Write about how you got on with the challenge below.

_____

_____

_____

_____

_____

_____

WEEK 39: SETTLE DOWN – PROBLEM

Teaching your dog to settle

I am reminded of the importance of teaching your dog this, when I see a post on social media along these lines: "Hello everyone, looking for more mind games to keep our boy (16 months) entertained. We walk, play fetch, play ball hockey and do obedience training. He uses lick mats and **Kong** with frozen food/treats. Any other fun tricks or 'jobs'? He's our first Border Collie." My immediate reaction is "**teach him to settle down!**"

That's a bit unkind, so I didn't say it, but it is definitely something you need to ensure your dog can do. Puppies can be very busy, on the go, around and about, all day every day. If you let them, this can become a 'lifestyle choice' and they just keep on going. Border Collies in particular, may struggle to relax, but that doesn't mean they can't do that!

Getting started

Please don't think the only way to **settle your dog down** is to shut him away? The best way to have your dog be calm and relaxed is to spend time with him, being calm and relaxed. This doesn't necessarily mean cuddling on the sofa, because not all dogs like to cuddle. Just be with them, not doing anything and not interacting with them.

Some dogs resist encouragement to settle and keep on finding toys to play with, bringing them to you. It's absolutely fine to play with them for a bit, or for them to play with each other. But they must learn that when you say 'finished', it's time to settle down.

Sleeping or settling

Dogs naturally sleep for around 14 hours per day, puppies for longer. So they should spend a great deal of the day asleep. I used to feel guilty if I had to go out for a few hours, which I rarely do. Then I realised that if they are left in peace, dogs usually just sleep.

If you are struggling to get them to stop, you may need to enforce it. This might mean putting them in a crate or run, at least to start with. You don't have to leave them alone though, just make sure they have some space. This is essential for young puppies, who need time out, particularly with **young children**. A tired puppy becomes very bitey!

Training a settle

Just as with any other training, it is possible to teach your dog to settle down. First of all, put them in a down and reward that. This should be at your feet, with you seated. Stroke your dog and talk quietly and calmly to them. You can try pushing them over, so that they lie flat, but only if they tolerate this.
Keep going, bringing them to you, lying them down, talking calmly, saying 'settle', until they relax and stop trying to get up and rush off. You can reward with a treat, but really, the reward should be just a bit of fuss.

Playtime!

Of course they are not going to settle all day long! Dogs do have playtime and they do have a 'crazy half hour' (or more) where they zoom around the room, bouncing off the furniture. They love to have toys to play with and will engage with you, playing tuggy or fetch. I find that my dogs will do this when we are trying to watch TV. I don't mind, because I know they are happy and stimulated. For a short time.

Don't forget though: **IT IS NOT POSSIBLE TO TIRE OUT A BORDER COLLIE!** So yes of course go for a lovely long walk every day, with plenty of time off lead. Spend time training or playing with your dog. Give them tasks to do, or **interactive toys**. But never, ever expect them to be 'too tired'. That is NOT a **breed characteristic**. Lol. Whatever breed of dog you have, the aim is to have a relaxed, happy dog, up for anything, but able to chill out.

Weekly Focus Challenge

How well does your dog settle down? If they are a Labrador, you probably don't know what I'm talking about! If they are a small dog who loves to bark at anything and everything, you might find this a bit of a challenge! Think about when your dog sleeps and when they are relaxed. What can you do to help them and improve their ability to relax? Notice how much better they are when they have been given a chance to chill out. Practice sitting calmly with your dog. It's good for you too!

Share a picture of your dog being good. Write about how you got on with the challenge below.

WEEK 40: SHOWING – INFORMATION

Showing your dog, as a dog activity

I had a lovely chat with my friend Nikki yesterday, when she was visiting to see the Punk Litter, with their grandad Sox and uncle Dreema. She explained to me how she got into dog showing and what she enjoys about it.

Pedigree Border Collies are not the most obvious breed for dog showing. However as they remain within the top ten breeds in the UK, it seems logical that they will be present at dog shows. This year (2022), a beautiful Border Collie was in the Best in Show competition.

Why did you choose to start showing with your dogs?

Nikki says *"I'd already been competing in agility and wanted to try something different. I thought my dog Sox's conformation was lovely and after reading the Breed Standard I wanted to see how he would do in the showring. I wanted a more sedate activity. I thought it would be a stimulating activity for the dog."*

Nikki has been showing for around ten years, but she says it took quite a while to get going. She had watched Crufts and thought it looked really easy. Then she realised that she had to get the best out of her dog, getting him to stand and focus on her, often for quite a while. It took a few shows to see that it takes a bit of practice.

What is the governing body for dog showing?

The Kennel Club is the organisation that manages most dog shows. They say *"Dog showing or exhibiting is an exciting competitive activity where dogs compete against each other for prizes or awards. It is a competition where a dog's attributes and conformation are compared against a breed standard for its breed. Whilst it can often be taken very seriously, it can be a fun pursuit that people and their dogs thoroughly enjoy."*

What types of dog show are there?
The following are the different shows you can enter:

- Companion dog shows
- Limited shows
- Open shows
- Premier shows

- Championship shows

Companion shows are a great introduction to dog showing, as they are informal events, usually part of a charity fete. They may have classes for pedigree dogs, but more commonly have classes such as:

- waggiest tail
- best trick
- golden oldie
- best pair of dogs, or family of dogs
- prettiest eyes

Other dog shows are only open to pedigree dogs. Limited shows consist of different classes for the different groups of breeds. Then there are different classes for dogs and bitches and for dogs of different age groups. The bigger the show, the more classes there will be.

What training do you need to do?

Initially, Nikki recommends attending a Ringcraft class. This will help you to prepare your dog, teaching them to stand correctly, move with you and to get used to being around other dogs. They will also advise you on which shows and classes to enter. Classes will introduce you to the format of the shows and how to behave when you are there.

You may also need to consider what physical activity you do with your dog, to keep them in peak physical condition. Swimming or physiotherapy are both recommended.

What equipment do you need?

Initially, you just need a show lead. This is a simple **slip lead**, which is not suitable for day-to-day use. You will need to train your dog to work in this lead, without pulling.

The main equipment needed is to do with making your dog looks its best. As Nikki says, you can spend thousands of pounds doing this! She says there are all sorts of tricks you can use to getting your dog looking great, with whiter hair, a smooth coat with a fabulous shine and so on. Nikki thinks **a hair blaster** is a must! She suggests talking to the stands at dog shows about the products available.

Other equipment includes crates and trolleys, grooming table and of course a variety of grooming tools.

What are the pros and cons of dog showing?

Nikki says *"I really enjoy getting them to move and getting the best from them. They love it."* However, it is not an activity for the faint-hearted. Nikki explains *"You have to remain objective, which is hard. You see another dog that you don't particularly admire win, while you are binned from the ring. It's all down to the personal choice of the judge. You have to keep your focus on your dog and enjoy showing them off. It's not about being competitive. It's a real test of character! Remember to congratulate the winners!"*

It is essential to remember you are taking the best dog home. For more information go to the **Kennel Club website**. Thank you to Nikki for sharing such interesting insights.

Weekly Focus Challenge

Do you fancy showing your dog? Find out about Ringcraft classes near you. Go along and watch initially, if you can. Or go along to a local fun dog show and see how it feels to have your dog judged by someone else. It can be useful to assess your dog alongside others; are they 'fit for purpose'?

Share a picture of your dog being good. Write about how you got on with the challenge below.

WEEK 41: SCENTWORK – TRAINING

Scentwork with your dog

Now that your dog is a year old, the fun really begins! You should be able to take them out and about without worrying too much about their behaviour. It's a great time to consider starting a dog activity – there are so many to choose from. I have a few to write about and I thought I would start with my newest interest – scentwork.

I started scentwork last September, mainly because my lovely agility trainer, Emma from Beancroft Agility, Scentwork and Hoopers, started teaching it! I also decided to do it with Ounce, as I wanted her to stop agility, for a variety of reasons. The main reason was that I just felt she didn't really love it and with plenty of other dogs doing it, there was no need for her to continue.

The basics

Dogs have an amazing sense of smell, everyone knows that. That sense is used in all sorts of ways, from finding people to sniffing out illnesses, or alerting people with medical conditions. Scentwork is the basic introduction to understanding how dogs use this amazing skill and harnessing it to do something fun.

Like most dog activities, (and most new skills) getting started is a bit slow and painful. But once you have the basics, it's amazing how quickly you can progress. It's lovely to see dogs of different breeds being able to excel at this activity. And of course it doesn't require much fitness or mobility from the handler.

The objective

Scentwork is all about working with your dog. Of course the dog knows where the scent is, but can you understand that? When you can go into a room, filled with obstacles and find the tiny marker with the scent on it, as indicated to you by your dog, that feels incredible. It's tricky though!

You begin by introducing one scent, which might be a rubber Kong, or a piece of cloth scented with cloves. The dog is shown the scent and then rewarded with food. And again. You keep doing this for a few weeks, until the dog understands that when they smell that scent, they get yummy treats.

Indicating

Once the dog knows what scent they are searching for, they have to be able to tell you where it is. This is taught slightly separately, but alongside learning what the scent is. You place a coin on the floor, wait for the dog to look at it, or sniff it, or touch it with their nose and say 'Yes!' and reward. And again. Keep going. You want the dog to understand that wherever the coin is, they should be looking at it, being still and waiting for you to say 'Yes!' (or use a clicker) and then they will get a reward.

Those are the two key skills that you and your dog need to have. Once your dog knows that they must find the particular scent and then indicate to you that they have found it, you can start to make real progress.

Scentwork in different places

It's a bit more complicated than that, but that's how you get started. Then it's about how you manage the dog, setting them up and making sure they look in the right places. Searches can be inside, outside, with a huge variety of different objects. Vehicle searches are carried out, along with searches of walls and doors.

What I like about this activity is that it's quite calm and relaxed, but it really challenges your dog. It's tiring and stimulating for them too! It also ensure that you really pay attention to them and watch their behaviour carefully.

Scentwork competitions

Scentwork UK run Trials around the country, if you wish to compete. These are structured around 8 levels, with each level including more complex and varied searches. So there is plenty to work on! If you fancy giving it a go, why not look for a trainer near you?

Weekly Focus Challenge

Do you fancy scentwork? Even if it sounds a bit serious, you might be surprised at how interesting and enjoyable it can be. If you don't want to do the formal training, you can still entertain your dog by playing hide and seek with a toy. If they will go and get a toy if you point at it or tell your dog to 'find it!' then you can try hiding a toy and asking your dog to find it. Listen to them sniffing? It's a really stimulating exercise for them. Make sure that your dog has time to wander and sniff on walks – don't march them along on lead at your pace, please?

Share a picture of your dog being good. Write about how you got on with the challenge below.

WEEK 42: OFF LEAD WALKING – PROBLEM

Walking off lead

Don't punish your dog with your laziness? That's harsh, I know. Please ask yourself, why your dog should be sentenced to a life of doing the same shitty walks, on lead, because you haven't bothered to build your confidence and let your dog off lead? Honestly, there is no excuse good enough for me.

Reasons for going off lead

Why should you bother? Simply:

1. It's more **stimulating for the dog** – you don't have to stop every 10 seconds whilst they sniff something
2. Being off lead is far **better exercise** – your dog will typically travel 3 or 4 times as far as you do, if they are off lead
3. It's safer – your dog can **move away** from anything they are not happy about.

I understand, it's really challenging. And scary, really scary, letting your dog wander about without you being able to immediately control them. Things will definitely go wrong. That's life. Don't ruin it for your dog by restricting them their whole life? Here are the excuses and my responses. You may not like them…

My dog will get attacked

Dogs do get frightened. The more you worry, the more likely they are to be afraid, bark and be attacked. Dogs do not necessarily want to **play or be friends with every dog** they come across. That's fine. You are there to watch out for them. Call them to you and either hold onto them, pick them up or just get their attention and reward them, as other dogs go past. Or let them look, sniff and wander over. Just observe and pay attention to the interaction. It's fine.

Ideally, you want the other owner to also be paying attention and understanding what is happening. It's no good saying 'My dog is friendly' if they other dog is clearly frightened. That's really annoying! But if your dog barks at another dog and you call him, apologising and getting hold of him, it's fine. Isn't it?

I appreciate that small dogs are more vulnerable, but they are also more aggressive and annoying! If they wind up a big dog, they might get eaten! Watching them and calling them away should still work though. When a big dog is off lead and can get away, there isn't much of a problem. All of this problem can just as easily happen with dogs on lead. In fact, dogs on lead are much more aggressive than those off lead.

My dog is scared of everything

'Reactivity' in dogs is hard to live with. You want to protect your dog from the big scary world and the easiest way to do this is keep them on lead. Ultimately, many people find it too stressful walking a dog that is frightened of other dogs, or bikes, or cars. Sadly, some of these dogs never go off lead and often end up not being walked at all.

You can often fix this problem, with patience and persistence. As the owner of a barking, scared dog, I know that it is really challenging, but I persist in walking him off lead. On some days, I walk where (and when) it is much quieter, so we don't have to deal with it at all. I've also found that walking in woods means the dogs we meet are more laid back and are also off lead, so it is much less of an issue.

My dog will run off

He might. Start by calling your dog *at home*. Does he come back? Did you reward him? Was there play and excitement from you? Have you practised recall hundreds of times? You should be able to understand your dog and his motivations, so that you know when he might run off.

Lots of people say their dog will come back fine, until there is a distraction, such as another dog, or a squirrel. True, but it's still possible to get them back, with enthusiasm, rewards and practice. Of course, some dogs get the scent of a squirrel or a deer and are off! They will run for miles, chasing something. Scary! I can't really comment on what it is like to own a dog like this, but when I go to the woods, there are plenty of Spaniels and Hounds of all shapes and sizes, running around off lead. So it must be possible.

My dog will get lost off lead

Some dogs do get lost. I've lost some of mine, over the years. Fortunately, they are required by law to wear a dog tag, with the name, address and phone number of the owner clearly shown. I recommend a flat 'Indigo' tag, instead of a dangly one, although stupid people may not find this. If you have an old dog who does wander, how about a lovely yellow tabard with your number on it? You can also now buy a tracking device for your dog – ideal.

Fortunately, we are also now required to **microchip** our dogs, so if they are lost, they will be found and sent home. People are pretty caring. Social media is full of dogs being found and then reunited. It works, hurray.

My dog will get run over

Yes they might. If you walk beside a road and pay no attention to your dog. I have had one of my dogs hit by a car and it was awful. We were crossing a road, with 5 dogs off lead and one (Sunny) went before I was ready and bounced off the wheel of a car. I was lucky, because she suffered no injury at all, although the vets kept her in for observation.

Did this stop me crossing roads with my dogs off lead? No, it did not. I'll put the youngest on lead for a year or so, but I just pay close attention and manage them. I don't recommend doing this, but it is possible. I don't normally walk beside a road with them off lead. You have to do a risk assessment and decide what is right for your dogs.

Generally though, off lead is always better than on lead. If you keep your dog on lead, they are living a poorer life. In my opinion.

Weekly Focus Challenge

Do you let your dog off lead? What are your reasons for doing or not dong this? Please, please, please find a way to have a go at this? Trust your dog? They will thank you. If you don't feel comfortable doing this on your usual walk, why not try a different walk? Or go to one of the growing number of 'secure fields'.

Share a picture of your dog being good. Write about how you got on with the challenge below.

_____

_____

_____

_____

_____

_____

_____

WEEK 43: HEALTH TESTING – INFORMATION

Health testing for better dogs

There is a strong 'movement' for people to 'adopt don't shop' for dogs. You are told to get a dog from a rescue centre and not from a dog breeder, or 'greeder' as we are often called. I'm revisiting this issue to talk about the value of health testing in dogs.

We do health tests to prevent possible suffering and illness. This is no different from taking our blood pressure, or doing a blood test to check our cholesterol levels. We take preventative medication ourselves, so why wouldn't we want to do that for our dogs?

Pedigree or crossbreed – which is healthier?

I've seen a great deal of anger about the fact that pedigree dogs can have huge health issues. Yes, that's true. But what you may fail to realise is the **just because a dog is a pedigree, that does NOT mean they have been bred responsibly, for better health.**

The definition of a pedigree dog is one with two parents of the same breed. Insurance companies call a labradoodle bred from two labradoodle dogs a pedigree. The parents are known to be specific crossbreeds and they are the same. However, that has nothing to do with a pedigree as defined by the Kennel Club. For this organisation, a pedigree is a dog that conforms to the Breed Standard for that breed. Even then, that dog may not be the healthiest they can be. That is down to the way it is bred.

Why health test

For me, health testing is part of the process of making sure our dogs are as healthy as possible. I feed the food I believe is best for my dogs. They are exercised the right amount for their age and development. I engage them with training. My dogs are vaccinated every year, to prevent them suffering from common, preventable disease.

If you don't care about 'papers', or where your dog has come from, that's your choice. Sadly, that means your dog may have started life in a tiny pen, in the dark, in a barn, with little or no human contact. It means your dog may have come from a mother who was repeatedly bred from. Or your dog may have been brought here from another country, either legally or illegally.

A better life?

It's fantastic if you take on a dog that has had a poor start in life and give them a better life. That's great, because all animals deserve this. But I believe it's better to have a dog that has been bred *on purpose.* This means talking to a breeder, placing an 'order' and waiting, hopefully until the puppy you want becomes available. It might take a long time.

Taking a chance

If there are health tests available, why take the chance? I would prefer to have a dog that has been tested? Organisations like the **Royal Veterinary College** are continuing to do fantastic research into health conditions, adding to the lists of tests that can be done. And the Kennel Club are taking this on board, adding to the list of **health test requirements and recommendations**.

Continued improvement required

Finally, just a comment about the fact that an obviously unhealthy Bulldog won Best of Breed at Crufts this year, 2022. I challenged the Kennel Club about this and received an interesting response. The Kennel Club say they are continuing to work hard to reduce this type of judgement being made in showing, but that the judge on the day makes their own decisions.

They say they are improving breed standards and health testing requirements for the Assured Breeder Scheme, but that not all dogs entering the showing classes have to conform to these standards.

The response I received stated:
"The Kennel Club, as part of the Brachycephalic Working Group up – Working together to improve the health and welfare of brachycephalic dogs (ukbwg.org.uk), has been working to change perceptions about what should be normal and desirable when looking for flat faced dogs. Changes to entire breeds – inside and outside the show ring – will take time to surface but we urge puppy buyers to see the puppy's parents to look for more moderate examples of these dogs, and to also look for dogs that have been tested for potential breathing difficulties."

The Kennel Club say the following about the Assured Breeders scheme: **We're the only organisation accredited by the United Kingdom Accreditation Service (UKAS) to certify dog breeders under our Assured Breeders scheme.** The scheme is intended to help direct puppy buyers to breeders who follow best breeding practice and conduct health testing for known inherited health conditions in their breeds. **Find out more about the scheme** and how to join.

I have written about health testing many times already, including one of the pupdates from last year's litter.

Weekly Focus Challenge

What health testing did the parents of your puppy have? Were these tests required for the breed or breeds? Do you have copies of the test results? Did the breeder explain these tests and why they are done? If you have a rescue or crossbreed, try to find out what health tests your dog's parents could have had? Be aware of genetic issues and what that might mean for your dog's health?

Share a picture of your dog being good. Write about how you got on with the challenge below.

WEEK 44: HOOPERS – TRAINING

Hoopers or agility?

I have already talked about **Hoopers** as a **dog activity**, but I thought I would put a more personal spin on this activity once we had started training Quin. I say 'we' because my husband Chris is going to be responsible for this bit of training! He injured his knee a few years ago running Luna in agility and had to retire. Hoopers is great alternative for him to try.

I am indebted once again to Emma from Beancroft Agility, Scentwork and Hoopers, who started teaching Hoopers last year. It's a great way to get Quin ready for **agility**, without impacting his joints too early. And who knows? We may decide that Hoopers is more fun anyway!

Getting started

There are four main pieces of equipment in Hoopers: hoops, tunnels, barrels and mats. Once the dog understands the need to look for these items and run over, through or round them, they can really get going! So as with so many aspects of dog training, you start by teaching your dog that these things have 'value'. In other words: ***Do this and you get a reward!***

It is amazing, watching dogs learn. Especially dogs of different shapes, sizes, breeds and ages. You can teach an old dog to do hoopers. They will still 'work' for a reward. Well you will still work for a reward, won't you? (I'm talking about chocolate.)

You can start by 'luring' the dog to go through the hoops or tunnels, but it is much better for the dog to figure out what is required and then get a reward for doing it. This is called '**shaping**'. You need to set the dog up to succeed, by standing right next to the equipment and look where you want the dog to go, rather than looking at the dog. When the dog moves, you throw the food where they are going. And again.

Progressing hoopers

Once the dog understands that they must look for the equipment, you can start to build up simple sequences. It doesn't take long for this to happen – a few weeks – but you must be patient and consistent. Keep **rewarding**!

Hoopers courses are fast and flowing, along smooth lines, with curves rather than sharp turns. It's about the dog moving easily and with minimal impact. It's also about you being able to direct your dog from a distance – no running required!

Young and old dogs

Whether or not you do plan to go on to do agility, hoopers is a great way to engage a lively young dog. You need to be able to set them up and move away, so a good wait is essential. Ideally, they should be motivated to play with a toy as well, so that you have plenty of ways to reward. It is exciting! It is a useful way to build fitness and control whilst moving at speed.

For older dogs, it's a great way to ease them into retirement from agility. Up till now, people retiring old dogs from fully competing to entering an 'Allsorts' class. This still involves jumping though, albeit at a lower height. Hoopers uses many of the skills learnt in agility, but without the twists and turns, or the impact. And if you only have an older dog, it's not really worth going to an agility show for a couple of classes, with no grades, or rewards for places.

Left and right

One of the skills you do need to teach a dog for hoopers (and agility) is left and right. Did you know that dogs know left and right? In order to teach this, I find it helpful to start by telling them 'left' or 'right' as they come to a turning on a walk. If it's a route they know and you give the command as they turn, they begin to associate the two things together.

Amazingly, if you practise this often enough, when you shout 'left' or 'right' your dog will then turn in that direction. You'd better just hope you shouted the correct word! Having a good range of commands will help you work your dog from a distance, which is one of the key aims of this activity. This in turn will really help you when you make the switch to agility. Of course your old agility dog will ace this aspect of hoopers!

Hoopers competitions

Canine Hoopers UK do run competitions, but as the sport has only being going for a few years, these are not widely available. The nice thing about these competitions though is that, unlike in agility, they are quiet affairs, with a great deal of effort being made to help young or reactive dogs.

Hoopers can be seen as 'a bit tame', compared with some dog sports, (agility again!) But it is still fun to work with your dog to achieve a range of different goals. There are levels to work through and rewards (rosettes) for doing so. Whatever you do, it will be fun with your dog!

Weekly Focus Challenge

Do you fancy giving hoopers a go? Why not find out if you have a trainer near you? Local groups on social media are a great place to ask for recommendations.

Share a picture of your dog being good. Write about how you got on with the challenge below.

WEEK 44: FIRST BIRTHDAY – CELEBRATING!

Birthday Boy!
What an amazing year it has been with this boy! Sometimes things just work out a certain way and I am so glad they did this time. There was a bit of juggling around with the homes for this litter and we ended up with him. So here we are, celebrating Quin's birthday.

Quin has such a great temperament. He's calm in so many situations, being far more laid back than many Border Collies. He loves people and will happily go up to anyone to say hello and have a fuss. Although he doesn't jump up, he does like to give 'one lick' to say hello!

I have taken Quin up and down the country; he's been to Scotland and South Devon. He always copes with new experiences perfectly. That is why I had him assessed to start volunteering, supported by Canine Concern. We love visiting Heronsgate Junior School and he often makes the children laugh!

I've tried a few different activities with Quin, including tricks, scentwork and now hoopers. I expect to continue with at least one activity with him in future, as I love having time with my dogs on their own.

I plan to put him to stud, so we will start completing the various health tests shortly. And I have almost completed the blog I have been writing, since he became 'our' puppy, at 8 weeks of age. You can read Quin's Story on the Dentbros Dogs website.

Happy birthday too to his siblings, the rest of the Mystical Litter! I am lucky enough to have seen three of them on more than one occasion, and I am in regular contact with all of them.

Weekly Focus Challenge

Have you celebrated your dog's birthday? Did you do anything special for him?

Share a picture of your dog being good. Write about how you got on with the challenge below.

WEEK 45: BREED TRAITS – PROBLEM

Different breed temperament traits

It might seem strange to talk about breed traits now, when you have had your puppy for so long. But I think that until you really get to know your dog, it's sometimes hard to understand what their character is like. How much of this is down to their breed? What will you be able to fix or what will you have to live with?

Traits in popular breeds

Someone recently said to me that they found their dog could be quite nervous in new situations and was often quite shaky. It was a poodle, so I said 'yes poodles tend to do that'. She was so surprised, because she wasn't aware that it was one of that breed's traits. So what other traits can we identify? How much is your puppy typical of its breed?

If you have a Labrador, you will know that they are laid back, easy-going and generally hoover up all food (and often non-food items) lying around. They are so lovable, which is why they remain one of the most popular breeds. But Labradors are also perfectly trainable and can hold down responsible jobs, most notably as Guide Dogs for the Blind.

Which group of breeds?

When considering what type of breed traits, or characteristics you would like in your dog, start off by thinking about the different dog breed groups. These are best described on the Kennel Club website, along with breed descriptions for all 222 breeds recognised by them. There are 7 breed groups:

- hounds
- toys
- pastoral
- utility
- terriers
- working
- gundogs

Each of these groups of breeds will have different breed traits. If you have a terrier, such as a **Parson Russell**, or Jack Russell, you should expect them to be tenacious, lively and demanding. A bit of an awkward sod in other words!

Or officially *"Bold and friendly; a confident, energetic and happy dog that has the ability and conformation to go to ground."* That means they will disappear down a rabbit hole, given the chance!

Easy to live with?

If you want your dog to be easy to live with, you need to pay attention to these breed traits. Many small dogs are much more inclined to bark at everything! Whereas bigger dogs can be more placid and less reactive.

All dogs need **walking and time off lead** to explore with their noses, at their own pace. Some breeds will be far more energetic and demanding than others though. So you need to account for that when you consider the breed traits. If you want a couch potato, a **greyhound** is a great option!

What traits can you change?

I've already talked in detail about **temperament** and how this can be a mix of nature and nurture. You need to think about what you have achieved so far and how much you will be able to change.

With Quin, I know he is a typical Border Collie. So I know that he won't change much now. Like many of his breed, he can be anxious around other dogs, which makes him bark. I'm probably stuck with that now. So we just have to manage that and make sure it doesn't get worse.

Mixed breed, mixed traits

I will just say, as I always do, that if you have a combination of breeds, you will have a combination of traits. So you won't know exactly what sort of dog you are getting and it probably won't be until you've had them a year that you can start to recognise which bits are from which parent (or grandparent).

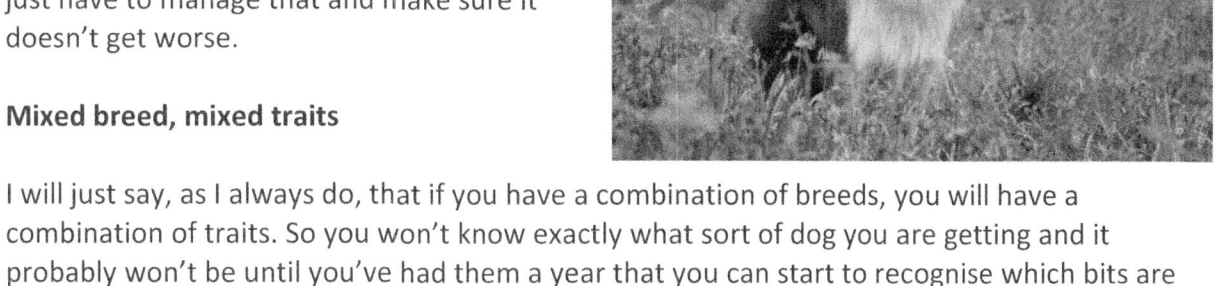

For example, if you have a cockerpoo, you may get a bright dog, that is a bit shaky and clingy, but also full of energy and very demanding. Actually, it's pretty likely that that is what you've got! What do you think, is that ideal? They might look like a teddy bear, but are they confident and outgoing, easy to take out and about? Or do they bark and run off?

Weekly Focus Challenge

Is your dog typical of its breed? Are they what you were expecting? How well do they match up to your lifestyle? What do you wish you'd done differently in choosing your dog? Would you get another one of the same breed?

Share a picture of your dog being good. Write about how you got on with the challenge below.

WEEK 46: DOG HEALTH – INFORMATION

How good is your dog's health?

Beautiful Border Collies, bred for better temperament and health. That's the tagline for this website and it sums up my ethos as a breeder. The health of my dogs is VERY important to me and above all, I want to produce dogs that go on to have long and happy lives.

When I talk to prospective owners I ask them 'what is the best and worst thing about owning a dog?' For me, the worst thing by a mile is coping with a sick and dying dog. It's absolutely heart-breaking. Perhaps it won't surprise you to know that I monitor the health of all the puppies I've produced, recording all their health issues, as far as I can.

How often do you go to the vet?

I've also been keeping a record of all my vet visits for the last five years. I've been 59 times! Wow those vets must love me. Let me break that down a bit more:

- I've had five dogs throughout that time and now have six. So that's around 12 times per dog.
- Luna was diagnosed with diabetes after losing her litter, so has been 23 times. She has to be regularly monitored, with blood tests and glucose curves. She has never had a 'crisis' and her diabetes continues to be well-managed, despite her now being 12 years old.
- 27 visits have been for vaccinations. Routine, annual check-ups.
- Sunny was 11 years old five years ago and suffered from arthritis, for which she had medication for a while. She also had pyometra, which involved an emergency operation. She was taken ill and was put to sleep last March, aged 15 (3 visits).
- I've had 5 litters over the past five years. Two of the girls, (Aura and Busy) have now been spayed.
- This total does not include visits for health testing, such as eyes and hearing.

Without the diabetes and the routine vaccination visits, that's only 9 visits in 5 years! Maybe I've missed a few, but actually, that's not far off. Pretty amazing isn't it? Thanks to **Milton Keynes Veterinary Group** for their care of my animals.

Be prepared

Most people insure their pets, although this is not a legal requirement. Is it worth it? I can't answer that, because I have never insured my pets. I'm fortunate to have enough money to pay for vet bills and with multiple dogs, the premiums would be enormous.

Whether you insure them or not, be prepared for them to be ill. They will definitely be ill during their lifetime! Sadly, some breeds are much more prone to illness and health problems than others. Someone recently said that they wouldn't get another Labrador, because the one she'd just lost had had cancer. I've spoken to a couple of vets since then, who agree that Labs are one of the healthiest breeds you can have. As long as their hips and elbows have been checked before being used for breeding.

Breed health issues

Sadly, some breeds have inherent health issues. Most notably the brachycephalic breeds, such as the Pug, or any kind of bulldog. I've already talked about the poor bulldog at this year's Crufts and what the Kennel Club are doing about it.

There are lots of breeds that can live fit, healthy, happy lives. Top tip: Get a dog that looks like a dog! The more this animal is distorted, the more likely they are to have problems.

"One way of reducing your pet insurance bill is to avoid dog breeds that attract higher premiums, such as Great Danes, French Bulldogs or Chihuahuas. Research by Which? consumer group found choice of breed made a difference by as much as £450 to an annual premium."
Financial Times

Living a long life

Generally, dogs live for around 10-12 years. However, this will vary according to many factors. A recent paper published by VetCompass shows that brachycephalic breeds like the French Bulldog live on average for just 4.5 years, compared to Border Collies, who live just over 12 years, on average.

TAIL OF THE TAPE... HOW LONG THEY LIVE

Breed	Years	Breed	Years
French bulldog, left	4.53	Cavalier King Charles spaniel	10.45
English bulldog	7.39	Shih Tzu	11.05
Pug	7.65	Cocker spaniel	11.31
American bulldog	7.79	Staffordshire bull terrier	11.33
Chihuahua	7.91	Labrador retriever	11.77
Husky	9.53	Mixed breed	11.82
Beagle	9.85	Springer spaniel	11.92
Boxer	10.04	Border collie	12.1
German shepherd	10.16	Yorkshire terrier	12.54
		Jack Russell terrier, bottom left	12.72

This statistic is skewed by high puppy mortality in some breeds compared to others. I've only had one puppy die soon after birth. Of the remaining 64, all but three are still alive, with six of my first litter of seven pups still going. Hopefully that will continue..

If you want to improve your dog's life expectancy, read my **7 tips on being a brilliant dog owner**. Or read the article on the Collieology Facebook group.

Weekly Focus Challenge

How healthy has your dog been so far? How many times have you been to the vet? Has it been worthwhile having your dog insured? Would you be able/prepared to pay £5000 to treat a complex medical condition?

NB: Remember that people don't become vets to make lots of money. They do it because they LOVE animals. If your dog has been poorly bred or raised, or has genetic problems, that is your problem.

Share a picture of your dog being good. Write about how you got on with the challenge below.

WEEK 47: AGILITY – TRAINING

Doing agility with your dog

Agility is my passion and one of the (many) reasons I have Border Collies. I loved watching it at Crufts growing up and when I got Sunny, it was always my intention to do agility with her. Little did I know how hard it would be! I've learnt more about myself doing agility than doing anything else in my life. Honestly.

I have written an introduction to agility on my website and I don't really intend to cover that ground again here. I will just repeat the stated 'objective' here:

"Have fun with your dog! It is vital to remember this, because agility is hard! In competition, the objective is to get your dog round a course of 16-20 obstacles in the fastest time. Easier said than done!"

Beginning agility

Don't start too soon! I have delayed writing about it because it's really important not to do too much too soon. It is a high impact sport and can easily lead to injuries for both you and your dog, if not done sensibly. You definitely do need a reasonable level of fitness yourself, especially if you want to get to the top level.

Your dog also needs to be able to move freely and easily. It's no good going if your dog is overweight, or can't run around for long periods. They should be around a year old when they start, so that their joints have had time to finish growing and developing. There is training you can do before you start, but the dog should not be jumping at all in their first year.

You need an experienced trainer, with a full set of proper equipment and ideally a good quality training area, either indoors or outdoors. I've always trained outdoors, but obviously you are then at the mercy of the weather, which can lead to weeks of training being lost.

How long does it take to learn?

I've been doing agility for 15 years now, but I only do a couple of hours a week. I've trained 5 dogs and all of them have had time off for puppies. Some people take to it really quickly, if they and their dog are young and fit. Other people get their own equipment, or become a trainer, spending many more hours per week training.

I'm a great believer in the fact that it takes 10,000 hours to learn a skill. That's a long time; I've probably done about 1500 hours so far... Of course I am not the only one doing agility – it's a partnership between me and my dogs. And they have NOT done ten thousand hours! Nor will they, sadly, because a dog's agility career will last for ten or eleven years, at best. Enjoy it while you can.

What's so great about agility?

Dogs love it. Generally. Some cannot see the point of expending effort just because you ask them to. **Border Collies** love to be doing something and they *love* to please you, so it is heaven for them. They love it *so* much that there are classes just for collies (NBC – Nothing But Collies,) and classes for everyone else (ABC – Anything But Collies). If you really want to avoid collies, you'll need a small dog, as Border Collies come in all shapes and sizes – Large, Intermediate AND Medium!

I love agility because I am competitive, so I like the challenge of improving and measuring that improvement. If I'd known how long that improvement would take to achieve, I might have started doing something easier, like knitting.

Why is agility so hard?

Dogs can't read numbers, so you have to tell them which way to go. Do you know your left and right? Can you run, wave your arms in a clear way AND shout directions? Are you able to remember a sequence of obstacles and work out which of the 8 possible ways to tackle these will work best for you and your dog? Do you run faster than your dog?

A year ago I went to an **agility show**, looking forward to demonstrating the skills I had worked so hard to acquire. The courses were set for the next level up, with skills that my dog and I did not have. I had no chance. It was an utterly demoralising experience. Last weekend I went to another show, full of dread and with no expectations. Busy bombed round, sometimes going over the right obstacles, but not necessarily in the right order. Aura and I perfectly executed the skills we had, over two entirely appropriate courses. We won. Twice. The satisfaction is indescribable.

Either way, the dogs had fun and I took the best ones home. Love my dogs. Love doing agility. Sometimes. Always grateful to my wonderful trainer, Emma Conlisk at Beancroft. For more information (and to enter a show) have a look at Agilitynet. Finally, for some real inspiration into what can be achieved, watch agility at Crufts, on one of the international competitions.

Weekly Focus Challenge

Do you fancy giving agility a go? Look for a reputable trainer via social media – ask in local dog groups. Go along and watch first; it's not like it is on the telly! Your dog will need to be fit and able to run around *before* starting agility.

Share a picture of your dog being good. Write about how you got on with the challenge below.

WEEK 48: TEMPERAMENT IN BREEDS – PROBLEM

Testing temperament

Following on from my post about health testing, in order to produce 'The dog of your dreams' it is also important to breed for temperament. Now I've had my dog for a year, I have been reflecting on his temperament and what makes him the way he is. Of course, he is a Border Collie, first and foremost, so his behaviour will always reflect that.

It is interesting to me that many of my 'dog friends' say to me things such as 'all your dogs are so good natured/well behaved/lovely temperaments'. They know about dogs and they think it significant that mine are all 'nice' dogs. Someone recently said "It's so good to come into your house and the dogs are just pleased to see you. There's no chaos, or fighting, or anything like that." When I first had a person come to look after them when we went away, she couldn't believe they all got on so well. So how do I do it?

Nature vs nurture

I'm a psychologist (in as much as it was my degree subject), so I understand the interplay between nature and nurture. It's easiest to think of it as the balance between being biologically programmed to behave a certain way, or being brought up to be like that. Of course it's not an either/or situation, both are crucial in creating the dog you want (or the person, come to that).

Starting with nature, I choose stud dogs from lines that I study and understand to be good-natured. I have tended to stick with the Goytre lines, because I know the temperament of these dogs is fantastic. However, I don't want my dogs to be too inbred, so I sometimes need to add different lines. This means I might end up with different temperaments.

Nurturing temperament

As I say all over this website, my puppies are given a brilliant start in life, with loads of positive experiences. They are cuddled every day, meeting plenty of people, including children. Puppies in my house spend time around dogs of different ages and temperaments, so they should cope better when they are out in the world.

That covers the first eight weeks, but after that, it is over to their owners to define their temperament. I have had dogs I've bred be nervous of children, because they haven't spent time around them, once they have gone to their new homes. So different experiences continue to have an impact.

Different characteristics

When I had the Rainbow Litter, I had one of the owners ask me about managing the 'herding instinct' that Ounce's brother was showing. "I've never had to manage that, mine don't really do that," I said. Then Ounce started herding off other dogs. Hmm, a new characteristic to manage! That litter are also real water babies – thanks to their lovely dad, Sox!

Not all my dogs are the same. I can see likenesses between them, but also differences. It's fascinating to see the traits develop. And to see the likenesses within and between litters. When I'm doing agility with Busy, people always say 'She's so fast!' to which I respond 'Just like her mum!'

Can you change it?

Dogs, like people are a mix of their biology and their upbringing. So you can influence how they are, up to a point. When I look at Quin, I can see he is a lovely nature. Like Busy, he's generally calm and laid back. But then he barks at other dogs, or something on TV! Funny boy. I've worked hard on the barking at other dogs and he's more or less stopped doing that. I think that yes, you can change their temperament, a bit.

It's complicated isn't it? I do my best to make lovely dogs – the dog of your dreams. Sometimes it goes it bit wrong (Aura :p). Oh she's lovely, I'm only kidding. Hopefully it's given you food for thought.

Weekly Focus Challenge

How is your dog's temperament? Has this changed much since they came home to you? What do you like about them? What would you change? Do you think you can change anything much about their temperament?

Share a picture of your dog being good. Write about how you got on with the challenge below.

WEEK 49: VACCINATIONS – INFORMATION

Vaccinations for your dog

We all know that puppies should be vaccinated, but how about ongoing vaccinations? There has been a growing and ever present 'anti-vaxxer' movement, which includes vaccinations for dogs, sadly. This preventative approach to serious disease has been around since Edward Jenner inoculated a 13 year-old-boy with vaccinia virus (cowpox), and demonstrated immunity to smallpox. In 1798, the first smallpox vaccine was developed. Dogs have been vaccinated for over forty years.

All vaccines carry a risk, but that risk of side effect is miniscule compared with the benefits. As the AAHA says *"No medication is without risk, but the benefits of vaccinating pets certainly outweigh the few risks because many common vaccinations in pets protect against devastating diseases, and even death."*

Puppy vaccinations

Traditionally, puppies were always sent off having had their first set of vaccinations. However, when I took Sunny along to be registered with a vet, they insisted on starting the process off again, as they wanted to be happy that she had been given the same type of vaccination, from the same 'batch'.

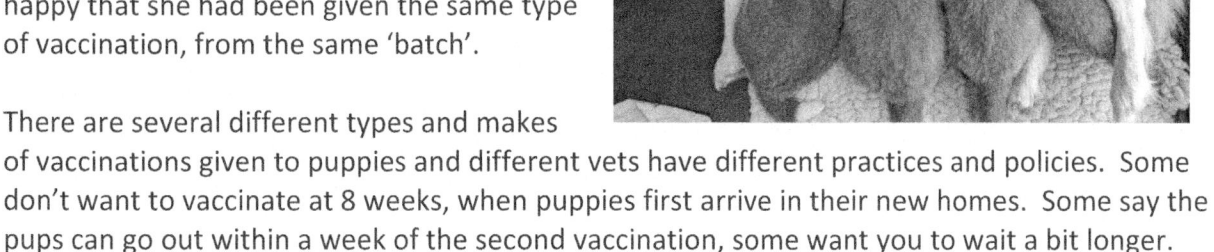

There are several different types and makes of vaccinations given to puppies and different vets have different practices and policies. Some don't want to vaccinate at 8 weeks, when puppies first arrive in their new homes. Some say the pups can go out within a week of the second vaccination, some want you to wait a bit longer.

Puppies are covered by the mother's immunity when they are being fed by her. These levels of immunity from the mother come from the first few days of feeding and this can last for variable amounts of time, from 6 weeks up to 20 weeks.

Your vet will start your puppy on a course of vaccinations against the four main infectious diseases:

- Canine Distemper
- Hepatitis
- Parvovirus
- Leptospirosis

All these diseases are fatal, so it is vital that your dog is protected from these. More details about what vaccinations should be given and when can be found at KC health advice.

Can you take my puppy out before they have been vaccinated?

Yes. You need to make sure they do not come into contact with dogs that have not had their vaccinations, or go someone where they might pick up these diseases. However, it is really important for pups to get out and about, as long as they are carried, or you know the dogs they are mixing with. It is great experience for your puppy and a chance to show them off to family and friends! Use a handy Pet Sling and off you go!

Ongoing vaccinations – how often should they be done?

Once again, times have changed. In the past, we accepted that we should vaccinate our dogs every year. However, we have come to realise that it is not necessarily appropriate to give our dogs *all* these vaccinations. Vets have discovered through scientific investigation that in fact the effect of the vaccinations last a bit longer than a year. They have therefore reviewed their policy for vaccinating.

My vet now carries out a rolling programme of vaccination. They vaccinate against leptospirosis every year, but other diseases are done every other year, or every third year. I have also discovered that the dogs are covered for up to 15 months. I therefore make sure that I don't now take them on the anniversary of their last vaccination, but wait until a bit later. That saves me money and makes sure that my dogs don't get done unnecessarily.

Alternatives to vaccination

Some people feel that they would rather treat their dogs another way, rather than 'over-vaccinating'. They might 'titre test' their dogs, which is a blood test used to determine the level of immunity in the dog's system. This is fine, on the day of testing, but it is not a reliable measure of the long-term cover the dog has.

I value the knowledge and expertise of my vet. I believe that they have spent years training and studying to understand what is best for my dog. It's easy to be critical of something you don't understand, but I would prefer to trust a professional person, than go through the hassle of learning all about it myself. I go to the **MK Veterinary Group** and I am happy with their service. People complain that vets charge too much money, but it must cost a fortune to run a practice, ensuring that they are ready and able to deal with everything that we throw at them. I think my Veterinary Practice is great!

Weekly Focus Challenge

I hope your dog has been vaccinated? It will be time for their first annual booster shortly. Check with the vet whether this needs to be done after 12 months or you can wait a bit longer?

Share a picture of your dog being good. Write about how you got on with the challenge below.

WEEK 50: SEPARATION ANXIETY – TRAINING

What is separation anxiety?

Separation anxiety is defined as when your dog shows signs of stress at being left, usually in the house on their own. The dog will often bark, or howl, sometimes for long periods. This may result in complaints from neighbours.

Can your dog stay calmly in another room?

Other symptoms can include repetitive behaviours, such as chewing their paws or over licking themselves. Or they might become destructive; chewing furniture or even the fabric of the house itself. Sometimes dogs become 'naughty' – soiling in the house, or pulling rubbish from the bin.

Quin used to chew cushions! It may seem obvious that these behaviours are seeking attention, but that doesn't make your life any easier! Basically, your dog is not happy without you.

Starting young

In order to avoid separation anxiety, you first of all need to develop confidence in your dog. They need to be certain of your love and your presence. You need to spend time with them, playing and petting them. If you have obtained a puppy from a KC Assured Breeder then they should be well socialised and used to normal family life.

When you get your puppy home, it might be tempting to spend all day, every day with them, or to take them with you everywhere. However, it is vital that your puppy is used to being left, right from the start. I always have a Crate for my puppies and they sleep in this, in the kitchen, from day one. They know that this is their bed and their safe space. The puppy should be rewarded every time they are put into their crate. Never use it as a punishment – if something has gone wrong, it was probably your fault!

Create calm

When you are in the house, try to encourage an atmosphere of calm. Easier said than done, I know! If you have children, there will inevitably be comings and goings, visitors and the normal hustle and bustle of family life. But try nonetheless to ensure that for some of the day at least, the dog is able to relax, while you are relaxed.

Reward the behaviour you want

When you see your dog lying calmly, reward them. The best way to do this is with a calm, gentle stroke and quiet verbal praise. You can say something like "Good settle, well done". The next stage is to have your dog calm and relaxed away from you, while you are in the house. Your dog might like lying at your feet, but they should equally be able to lounge around elsewhere. Some dogs actively seek other space – Sunny prefers to lie by the front door. Again, if this is a challenge for your dog, try leaving them for a few minutes, then return and praise. Gradually build up the time, until they are not fussing to come back to you.

Go out without them

It is hard for dogs to understand that you will be back. You cannot explain to them that all is fine and you'll be back soon. However, if you make it seem like no big deal, there is more chance that they will remain calm when you are not around. Try to avoid giving them a great big welcome when you come back – just walk in and get on with making a cup of tea. Then when you are settled, give them some love.

As with all training and behaviour, you must practice if you want success. So don't spend all day every day with your dog and then expect them to manage without you. Equally, going out to work for ten or twelve hours every day is a bit unfair on a dog. I used to think that no-one should ever work full time and have dogs. But I understand now that it is not that simple. Dogs naturally sleep for most of the day. So if they are given a walk or two, are able to go to the toilet every few hours (or have a run or yard to stay in), then they are probably fine. Equally, if you have more than one dog, they will interact with each other. **NB: I am not suggesting you get two puppies together!**

Provide stimulation

Dogs do need something to think about! In the wild they would be hunting for food, which they clearly do not need to do in our homes. Having said that, you can buy interactive feeding bowls that help the dog eat more slowly, or keep them entertained for longer.
You can also buy interactive toys for your dog. Although having a box of toys and a few bones to chew will provide plenty of stimulation. Empty yoghurt pots or drinks bottles can provide hours of fun!

Dogs do like company, but there are lots of options. I always leave the radio on when I'm out. If we are out in the evening, I might stick the TV on – lots of dogs watch TV. And dogs don't have to have other dogs for company; many dogs enjoy being around other animals, such as cats.

Finally, you can of course hire a dog walking service, who will come in and let your dog out, spend time with them or take them for a walk.

Weekly Focus Challenge

How well does your dog cope with being left? What do you do to help them when you go out? How often do you leave them? Is there anything you think you could, or should do differently?

Share a picture of your dog being good. Write about how you got on with the challenge below.

_____
_____
_____
_____
_____
_____
_____

WEEK 51: CONTACT WITH YOUR BREEDER

When to contact your breeder

In these days of reviews, ratings and feedback, it seems important to keep in touch with my customers and make sure that the 'products' I have produced are up to scratch. But people contact their breeder for all sorts of reasons and sometimes this is hard to deal with. So how much breeder contact have you had and has it been helpful and positive?

Star rating for Responsible Breeding

When puppies go off to their new homes, I give owners a 'New Owner Questionnaire' to complete and return to the Kennel Club. This has been done as a paper form to complete and post, but the Assured Breeder reps at Crufts this year told me that the Kennel Club are emerging from the Dark Ages to put this online. I suggested that breeders need feedback from the owners and that positive feedback could be done with 'star rating'. What do you think?

Please do contact your breeder? You have had your puppy for almost a year – how have they turned out? Are you pleased, or a bit disappointed? What issues or challenges have you had? What do you think they could have done better?

Please contact the Kennel Club Assured Breeder Service to provide feedback on the breeder. You should have been given:

- A Kennel Club Breed Registration certificate (did you change the ownership?)
- Information about endorsements to protect against future breeding
- A contract of sale, telling you to return the dog to the breeder at any point in the future
- Information to help you, including tips on socialisation, exercise, feeding, grooming, vaccination and diseases, as well as breed traits and tendencies.

You should have seen the puppy with its mother, being fed and interacting with its siblings. There should have been time to ask the breeder questions and see the breeder's dogs and the way they were kept. You should have been questioned about your suitability to have the dog.

The puppy must have been microchipped. If you feel that any of this was missing or not done well, please provide feedback? Of course if it was done well, that's equally good to know!

Initial support

When my puppies first go off to their new homes, I really love to hear how they are getting on. It's fantastic to hear that they have settled well, are behaving themselves and coping with their new lives. These days I set up a WhatsApp group for each litter, so that the owners can talk to each other, as well as to me. This has resulted in some owners becoming friends and meeting up, which is fantastic.

This also provides real support when things don't go quite according to plan! It's easy for me to jump in with 'helpful advice' but I do try to let owners talk to each other and share their experiences. Anyway, I don't always know the answer! I also have a Dentbros Puppies Facebook group for ALL the owners and lovers of my pups.

Ongoing breeder contact

Some people travel quite a distance to get their new puppy. **Finding the right breeder** is a real challenge, especially these days when puppies **bred responsibly** are in such short supply. After all, puppies are **not toilet paper**, as we should know!

So I don't expect to see all my puppies on a regular basis. I have been fortunate that many of my pups have gone to homes local to me, or to family or friends. That's wonderful, but not always possible. When they live further away, I don't expect to see them often, if at all.

Useful feedback

With most owners, I tend to only hear if there are problems. This can be relating to behaviour, or with health issues. It is really helpful for me to know if a dog I have bred is having difficulties. This might inform my decisions regarding breeding in the future. I also need to pass on any real concerns to the owners of the stud dogs I have used. Breeding for **'better temperament and health'** means constantly striving to improve the breeding of my dogs. Each generation should be better than the previous one. Healthier, with the right temperament for the breed and the homes the dogs are going to.

Breeding mentoring

Increasingly, people who own my puppies want to breed from them. They are wonderful dogs after all! This is a bit of a minefield for me, if I'm honest. I have built up years of knowledge and experience in breeding and believe I do it well. If people breed from the dogs I have produced, will they do it responsibly? I don't want people doing it 'just for fun', or because 'it's nice for the dog'. Consider the reasons not to breed from your dog, please?

If you do want to go ahead, you will need to start off by doing the necessary health testing for your breed. You should then talk to your breeder and ask them to mentor you. This can be really challenging as the breeder; you can end up feeling as though you have done all the work with none of the reward!

Proud of my puppies

The best feedback a breeder can get is to hear of their puppies' successes. Winning classes, in any dog activity, even if it is just for 'prettiest eyes' at a local dog show. It's brilliant to see a real partnership developing and I know that some of my puppies have the potential to go all the way with their owners. One day I hope that the Dentbros name will appear on TV, with a dog I've bred competing at Crufts, in the main arena!

I am equally proud to see healthy, happy dogs, living their best lives. Knowing that they are bringing pleasure to their families every day, doing the job they have been bred to do. So please contact your breeder to give this feedback as well?

We do have reunions, which is wonderful, although quite a challenge! Ask your breeder if they do this and see if you can meet the other owners from your litter – it's a lovely experience.

Weekly Focus Challenge

What did you think of your dog's breeder? How much contact did you have with them before collecting your dog? How much contact have you had since then? Has it been useful and positive? Would you like to meet up with other puppy owners from that litter?

Share a picture of your dog being good. Write about how you got on with the challenge below.

_____

_____

_____

_____

_____

_____

WEEK 52: CELEBRATING A YEAR WITH YOUR PUPPY!

Let's celebrate! It's been a year!
Well here we are! I am as surprised as you are that we have got to a year of owning a puppy! How's it been for you? As expected? Better? Or worse? What have been the highlights? What have been the unexpected challenges?

The year we've had

For me, the biggest, well really the only problem is the 'barking at other dogs'. He is still doing it and it is still driving me mad. I call him and he comes. He stops barking and says 'sorry mum I forgot'. Silly boy! I apologise and the other person says 'It's fine'. I say 'it's not fine, he's annoying.' We walk on. Oh and this morning he found some fox poo for his neck. Lovely!

Chris and I absolutely *adore* our boy – he's the best. We love how he barks at random stuff on the TV. It's so sweet to see him playing with Murmur and he's great with all the girls. He's such a goof. I love it when he snuggles up next to me on the sofa, chewing on a bone. And he's so handsome!

We think he's turned out pretty well. I feel confident taking him pretty much anywhere, as long as I watch him around other dogs. He's perfectly friendly (no really), meaning we can walk with friends or chat to people. He just likes to shout when he sees another dog.
Let's revisit the questions I asked you 6 months ago about your dog. Do you know them better now?

Around the house

1. What is your dog's favourite food? Are they a good eater? Do they need to be slowed down when eating? Nothing has changed with his eating and he continues to be fine.
2. What treats or snacks does your dog like? Raw carrot is a favourite of my dogs. They all love crisps and will offer lots of tricks to win these!
3. Where does your dog like to sleep? Do they go on the sofa or your bed? Or do they prefer to find a

quiet corner? I'm putting money on the fact they don't often sleep in that expensive bed you bought? My dogs like a raised bed with some lovely vet bed on it. They usually just lie on the floor, or the sofas, of course.

4. When does your dog wake up in the morning? What time do they go to bed? Does this work well with your routine? Your dog should be happier being left for longer periods, both day and night. What arrangements do you make when you are out?

5. How often does your dog need to go out to toilet? Do they always go in the same place? Do they prefer to toilet in the garden or on a walk? I like my dogs to be able to toilet in the garden, so that I don't have to take them out – it's so much more convenient. But I know they prefer to toilet on a walk. So I make sure I pick up after them in the garden as well as on walks and I walk them after breakfast so they can toilet then.

Out and about

6. How often do you take your dog out for a walk? Do you go at the same time each day? For the same length of time? My dogs have an hour long walk, off lead, around an hour after their breakfast, from 7.30 am.

7. Where does your dog like walking? Do you go to different places, or do the same trudge every day? Dogs love variety and thrive on visiting different walks. My dogs love the woods! So many interesting smells.

8. Where else have you taken your dog? Have they been to the pub? Or to a cafe? It's a good to show off your dog and give them a different experience. Quin continues to get out and about and enjoys the experience.

9. Have you visited someone else's home with your dog? Don't be afraid to take them into new situations? Quin has carried on going into school and behaves himself brilliantly (apart from barking at the chickens).

10. Have you taken your dog away? Quin has been up to Scotland and down to Devon – he loves it!

Tricks and games

11. Can your dog do the basics? Sit, down, wait? How often do you practise these? Every few days is a good starting point.

12. How is your dog's recall? How often do you practise this? Quin is perfect at recall – hurray! <smug>

13. Can your dog do any other tricks? We've done lots of tricks and Quin and I both really enjoy this.

14. What's your dog's favourite game to play with you? If you have other dogs, do they play together and what games do they play? Quin has a new playmate! He and Murmur play together a lot. So sweet.
15. Does your dog engage with other dogs when out on walks? Do they try and say hello nicely, or bounce into other dogs' faces? Still annoying. Not fixed. It's not the end of the world, but it is irritating.

Training and activities

16. What classes have you done with your puppy? Have you carried on with any classes? What did you learn?
17. Have you considered doing the KC Good Citizen Dog Training Scheme?
18. Have you tried out other types of training? Quin has started Hoopers, which he enjoys.
19. Now your dog is a year old, perhaps you could start agility?
20. Obedience training is another way to challenge you and your dog and build on your working relationship.

Health and breeding

21. What do you think of your dog's breed now? Has your dog continued to be typical of their breed?
22. How healthy is your dog? Have you been to the vet?
23. Have you had support from your breeder? Have you been in touch with the owners of your puppy's siblings? Each of my litters has a WhatsApp group, so they can share problems and celebrate successes!
24. Are you happy with way your dog was bred? Do you think they were given the best start in life? I have learnt that it makes a difference. A puppy that is cuddled every day likes being cuddled. It's that simple.
25. Is there anything about getting your puppy that you would do differently?

Enjoy your puppy now

Your dog may not be perfect, but they are part of your family. You have already had them for around a twelfth of their life. Think about what you were doing 11 years ago? Not long ago is it? That's how much time you have left. A year in their life is such a long time. Celebrate your puppy and the joy they have brought you.

Please take a moment to reflect on your successes and the remaining challenges? Think about what you'd like to do with your dog going forward? Please do get in touch if you'd like to share any of the answers to my questions?

Congratulations on surviving a year with your puppy. I hope it has been a wonderful, fulfilling experience, full of joy. I hope you have learnt a great deal about owning a dog and that you will help others to understand why owning a dog is one of the best things you can do in life. Please do contact me to let me know how it's been and what you have learnt?

Thank you for spending time on this workbook. Enjoy your puppy!
Penny

Weekly Focus Challenge

Please take a moment to reflect on your successes and the remaining challenges? Think about what you'd like to do with your dog in future? Please do get in touch if you'd like to share any of the answers to my questions?

Share a picture of your dog. Write about how you got on with the challenge below.

_____

_____

_____

_____

THE END

Printed in Great Britain
by Amazon